Because Dan
loved you, Will and
The Smith, Rachel

WILL CAMPBELL
and the Soul of the South

Thomas L. Connelly

WILL CAMPBELL
AND THE SOUL
OF THE SOUTH

CONTINUUM · NEW YORK

1982

The Continuum Publishing Company
575 Lexington Avenue
New York, N.Y. 10022

Printed in the United States of America

Library of Congress Cataloging in Publication Data

Connelly, Thomas Lawrence.
Will Campbell and the soul of the South.

Includes bibliographical references.
1. Campbell, Will D.   2. Baptists—Clergy—Biography.
3. Clergy—United States—Biography.   I. Title.
BX6495.C28C66   286'.132'0924   [B]   82-2334
ISBN 0-8264-0182-1   AACR2

Grateful acknowledgment is made to Sid Campbell for permission to reprint lines from
the song "Good Friday Morning" and to Glaser Productions for lines from "Mississippi
Magic."

For Barbara

Contents

✦

Preface

No one could write a formal biography of Will Campbell in the mode of a traditional biography. His life is not his alone, but is a symbol—if not an exaggeration—of the Southern way of thinking. Will Campbell's personal history is intertwined too closely with the soul of the South for us to separate the man from his heritage.

The enigmatic mind of the South is rooted in the concept of a soul set apart from the mainstream of American faith. The soul of Will Campbell and his region involves a different sense of time and place, a sense of history and memory that are apart from the national dream, and a peculiar civil religion grounded in a Stoic acceptance of evil and an optimistic Christian faith in the value of striving.

The cornerstone of this Southern faith exemplified by Will Campbell is a paradox of opposites which often appear to fluctuate wildly between extremes. At once Campbell's South is a land of violence and gentleness, fundamentalist religion and hedonism, literary excellence and illiteracy. There is an aura of hospitality, commingled with a suspicion of outsiders. The staggering number of parishioners in evangelical religions is matched by a high rate of homicides. The deep, humanistic bond between black and white people is counterbalanced by decades of racial turmoil.

Will Campbell embodies these paradoxes. The son of a poor Mississippi cotton farmer, ordained a Southern Baptist preacher while still a teenager, Campbell received a theological degree from the Yale University Divinity School. Everyone in Amite County, Mississippi, expected Campbell to come home, but he never really came back home. In the late 1950s Campbell became involved in matters that were far removed from his rural heritage and his Baptist ordination. There were years of activity in the civil rights movement where he was involved at critical moments in places such as Little Rock, Ole Miss, Albany, and Birmingham. Campbell was the only white man present for the organization of the powerful Southern Christian Leadership Conference. For years he worked in race relations for the National Council of Churches, and his friends there would not have been welcome in Amite County—Martin Luther King, Jr., Bayard Rustin, Andrew Young, and other activists. Surely Campbell was the prodigal son of a Mississippi upbringing.

In the 1960s, some of Campbell's liberal associates labeled him an outcast. During this time he drew nearer to his Amite County heritage, although he would never return to it completely. He began to champion the rights of all downtrodden people in the South, both black and white—even members of the Ku Klux Klan. Some things happened which led Campbell to lose faith in the ability of institutions—for example, churches and civil rights organizations—to solve human problems. Now Campbell views any institution, whether his native Southern Baptist faith or the National Council of Churches, as impediments to attaining the basic human kindness which underscores his personal religion.

Even today Campbell maintains "I am just a preacher," although in reality less than two years of his life were spent as a formal minister. His parishioners now cut across every dividing line of race, class, and creed. They are black and white tenant farmers, country-music singers, well-known American political and literary figures, the average citizens of his community of Mt. Juliet, Tennessee, academic theologians, and many others. He moves among them all, wearing his black padre hat, carrying a suitcase containing a bottle of bourbon and a New Testament, and his battered guitar case.

Always there is the guitar and country music. Sometimes Campbell sings the songs in college seminars and in formal church services; at other times he delivers his message to friends gathered around his kitchen table. For Campbell, country music is the thread which pulls together the patchwork quilt pieces of the Southern soul; it is religious music, the expression of a civil religion centered upon paradox, the acceptance of good and evil, strife, and failure.

Much of Will Campbell's own story is from that same oral tradition. The weeks I've spent with Campbell did much in retrieving his past and present attitudes. Some publications provided help. None was more valuable than his autobiography, *Brother to a Dragonfly* (New York: Continuum Books, 1977). Other books by Campbell which have provided assistance include: *Up to Our Steeples in Politics*, with James Holloway (New York: Paulist Press, 1970); *Race and the Renewal of the Church* (Philadelphia: The Westminster Press, 1962); and *The Failure and the Hope: Essays of Southern Churchmen*, edited with James Holloway (Grand Rapids, Michigan: William B. Eerdman's, 1972). In addition, much of Campbell's thinking can be found in his many essays in *Katallagete: Be Reconciled: Journal of the Committee of Southern Churchmen*. Another valuable source is *An Oral History with Will Davis Campbell, Christian Preacher*, volume 157 of *The Mississippi Oral History Program of the University of Southern Mississippi*, edited by Orley B. Caudill (Hattiesburg, Mississippi: University of Southern Mississippi, 1980). The best short analyses of Campbell are found in Marshall Frady, *Southerners: A Journalist's Odyssey* (New York: New American Library, 1980), "Fighter for Forgotten Men," also by Marshall Frady, *Life* Magazine, LXXII (June 16, 1972), and the excellent "Travels with Brother Will," by Mitchell J. Shields in the *Atlanta Weekly*, April 19, 1981. Above all, the best source is Will Campbell himself. Indisputably, he is the essence of the Southern soul.

PROLOGUE

At night the automobile headlights flash across the narrow pavement of U.S. Highway 31, which leads from the flatlands of Alabama and Mississippi into the bluegrass of Middle Tennessee. It is an old road, and it was aged even in 1864, when the Union and Confederate armies fought across the forty-mile expanse from Columbia, Tennessee, northward to Nashville. Now the old road takes me to a meeting with Will Campbell, and to my deeper understanding of the meaning of what it is to be a child of the South.

My own parents had moved from this area to Nashville during the years of the Great Depression, when Campbell toiled as a preacher in sweatbox Mississippi Baptist churches. Many families moved to Nashville during those years, leaving behind the so-called satellite counties which boasted of rich tobacco fields, cattle, and bluegrass. Some—such as my own father—lived out the aspirations of the archetypal achiever and became self-made businessmen along Little Wall Street on Fourth Avenue.

Years later I would understand that they had never really abandoned the rural land around Nashville because the bonds of family and community in the Southern mind cannot easily be uprooted. Ties with home and soil are not broken, only stretched. My own kind brought with them that deep, dark unyielding fundamentalist religious faith which today still dominates the culture of Nashville.

Preacher Will Campbell also had a rendezvous with Nashville. Although he did not know it, he would eventually be drawn to that city of paradoxes which is itself an exaggeration of the contradictions of the South. Nashville was my world for two decades, in what then would be regarded as an upper-middle-class neighborhood—called Oak Hill. Today the citizens of Oak Hill and contiguous Brentwood boast of the residences of many of the elite in the much-touted billion-dollar country-music industry—performers, songwriters, and publishers. Many are friends of Will Campbell.

The musicians began moving into Nashville's fashionable suburbs in the 1940s. There were changes in those southern winds which would later bring Will Campbell to Nashville: The Second World War and the social turmoil of its aftermath had fashioned a new South made up of transients—blue collar laborers in Birmingham steel mills, Appalachian migrants in Cleveland, workers in Houston oil fields, and thousands of others. They were not unlike Will Campbell who would also become aware of the tensions between his rural Mississippi Baptist heritage and the outside world. These people were rooted to the bonds of a Southerner's peculiar sense of family and community. In the 1940s they reached out for a new music—one to express the contradictions and strains in their own lives: the Southern Baptist credo, and drinking in a Cleveland tavern, the Southern preachments that marriages live forever, and divorce, and many more.

They were Ishmaels, caught somewhere between where they had been and now were—and country music expressed their passions. I knew part of this, as my automobile moved across the dark fields south of Nashville. My parents still lived in the boyhood home which stood on a Civil War battlefield. It was not far from a multimillion-dollar church where my father was a presiding officer. One of my brothers was minister to an affluent "white-flight" suburb on the southside, in an area where many who worked in the country-music industry lived. I was coming home, but it was not home at all. Long ago I had cast aside the rigorous religious fundamentalism. Many of my childhood friends were still there, living in the high Harpeth Hills south of town—good churchmen and civic leaders. I myself was a college professor in another state, divorced and no longer a believer in the old faith, one who suddenly felt light years away from the roots.

Perhaps this was why I had returned to Nashville to write a book on the culture of country music. I was intrigued not so much with the music alone, but with what it reflected of the overall patterns of Southern thought. Surely there must be a bond between the contradictory themes of the music—nostalgia and violence, expressions of Jesus's concern and laments of man's guilt, ballads of hope, mixed with defeat, in matters of love and money. I was puzzled also by how such music, which stressed the sensual and the physical, could prosper in Nashville, the undisputed capital of the South's Bible Belt.

But what resulted would become no book on country music at all, but a book on Will Campbell and the spirit of the South. It was to become part of a long learning, to understand that the music, the Southern mind, and the religion—even the culture of Nashville—were symbolized by Campbell. He was the Mississippi Southern Baptist preacher turned social radical; the civil rights leader who served communion to members of the Ku Klux Klan. He was the Yale-educated theologian who farmed thirty acres in a hollow near Nashville; the celebrated Southern author who sang ballads of the country folk; the lecturer on Ivy League campuses who ministered to the downtrodden in roadside taverns.

Putting disparate things like this together for other people seems to have become Will Campbell's calling. Sooner or later, a wide range of humanity makes the trek to his farm. His friends are country singers and politicians, civil rights leaders and theologians, prominent educators and ordinary farm people. He is a combination of sage, chaplain, and friend, particularly to the great and small of Nashville's Music Row. Famous singers, writers, studio musicians, and wanderers who never find their niche, all come to the hollow in the valley of the Stone's River, because Will Campbell epitomizes the Southern soul. He is, at once, all of the characteristics of a region: the paradoxes of alienation and love for one's heritage; the gentleness and the violence; the courage of striving and the long tradition of defeat. It is all in Campbell, and in the Southern mind. It is there in the music and in Nashville; it is all part of one faith.

Campbell's definition of that faith is that all people are literally God's children, whether black militants or Klansmen, country singers or Nashville businessmen. Christianity to Preacher Will is pure and simple compassion for the human condition, particularly for those who are alienated from what the world outside considers the "mainstream."

So his life has become intertwined with Nashville and with country music. It was not by choice so much as by need. Sometimes the musicians come to his farm in the rocky hollow in the early morning hours. To Campbell, these are some of the South's most alienated people—estranged from their religious heritage in rural Dixie and separated as well from the religio-economic culture which dominates Nashville. After all, Will Campbell too has become an Ishmael.

The understanding of his life began on the old road, as the headlights picked out the signs along Highway 31. It was a road rich in Southern alienation, past and present. Ahead through fields of bluegrass and in the dark, green hills a few miles south of Nashville were the communities of Franklin, Brentwood, and Oak Hill and the homes of the most prominent people in the country-music industry. They, too, may be Ishmaels, who work and live in a culture far removed from their neighbors, the affluent Nashville bankers, attorneys, and insurance executives.

Tonight the music people slept in their lavish homes built on the fertile fields. Beneath that land rested several thousand rebel soldiers who had fallen on the battlefields of Franklin and Nashville. They were outcasts in their own way.

These soldiers had marched along this old road in 1864, and I thought of them as the red-brick mansions and historical markers flashed by in the automobile's headlights. Across a field near the village of Spring Hill, I could see the lights of the Cheairs house. Some Confederate generals ate breakfast there one late-November morning in 1864, before they moved up the old road to die on the field at Franklin.

Highway 31 is almost a monument to the Confederacy's blasted dreams. Atlanta had been lost in a series of slaughters which historians term battles. The Army of Tennessee, the main rebel force on the western front, was led by General John Bell Hood, a handsome Kentuckian with a tawny blond beard, who had been the darling of Richmond's society. But his arm was shattered at Gettysburg, and two months later, his leg was blasted away on the field at Chickamauga. Then he lost the Atlanta campaign, and, even then, tormented by failure, he still envisioned dreams of glory: He would take the army home to Tennessee, then would cross the Ohio River and invade the Midwest.

I drove through Spring Hill past the old Peters' house. Earlier in the war, the flashy, yellow-haired rebel cavalryman, Earl Van Dorn, was shot to death in the kitchen there by a jealous doctor who believed the general was romancing his wife. Later, in the autumn chill of a late-November day, Hood's army tramped past the Peters' mansion in pursuit of a Yankee army racing them to Nashville. The skirmishing became heavier and casualties mounted. At the Peters' house, and others along the road, the Confederates dropped off their wounded, some of them screaming in the blood and ooze of those horrible abdominal wounds caused by the slug-like bullets of the sixties. Hood, strapped to his horse, pushed his men on to Franklin.

A few miles more, and my automobile climbed the long, cedar-laden Winstead Ridge overlooking Franklin. Off to the west is the old Harrison house. Jeanie C. Riley, a comely country honky-tonk singer, garnered her lot from a tune about myriad goings-on in small-town Dixie called "Harper Valley P.T.A." Now she lives in the brick mansion which served as a field hospital after the carnage at Franklin. General John Carter was mortally wounded just over the ridge, and bled to death in Jeanie C. Riley's home. From atop that ridge the lights of Franklin dot the bluegrass plain below. When I was a child, Franklin was one of those classic rural county seats where life centered around the courthouse and various businesses which sold cattle feed and farm machinery. Now it is the southern perimeter of the residential area of the country-music empire. Fancy shops peddle expensive clothing and saddlery.

A late-autumn wind blew across the ridge that afternoon as Hood's ragged army gazed down on the Yankee entrenchments at Franklin. Subordinate generals protested that attack would be suicidal, but Hood ordered the troops forward. They came with bands playing up Highway 31 past the modern Battleground Academy. Then the rebels struck the Union line near a home now called the Carter house. The brick walls are still pock-marked where bullets and shell fragments drove home. Out beyond the outdoor kitchen, young Captain Tod Carter was shot down in his own backyard.

Franklin was less a battle than a slaughter. Dead and wounded soldiers filled the deep ditches which lined the outside of the federal trenches. Some of the living gnawed their thumbs or bleated pitifully in their pain. In less than half a day, Hood's dream of reaching the Ohio River was shattered. His casualty list included 12 generals and 7,000 privates. Later they carried almost 1,500 corpses over to a plantation cemetery for burial.

The carnage at Franklin did not satisfy the deranged General Hood and he pushed his army on toward Nashville. My headlights picked up the southern approach to Holly Tree Gap where Hood's army trudged through the Harpeth Hills. Off to the left, in a hollow alongside Berry's Chapel Road is Tom T. Hall's stately home, reminiscent of an antebellum mansion. He named it Fox Hollow—though others have called it Tara Revisited.

Through the gap the road drops into the Little Harpeth River bottom. The old Wilson house, Mooreland, and other prewar mansions stand almost surrounded now by the clusters of lights defining the suburbs built by money brought in by country music. General Hood dropped off more sick and wounded at the old homes, and still more at Midway, off to the west of the highway. Today, Midway is the central structure of the Brentwood Country Club, where the new music money shares golf carts with the Nashville establishment.

At last I reached Brentwood, the shopping complex for the country-music empire. I grew up here long before it was the residential enclave of the music people. I attended Robertson Academy along with the children of the old Nashville "horse" set—the Sloans, Sharps, and others. Their fathers were the Nashville power brokers of the 1940s—the bankers and insurance executives who owned the lush, beautiful bluegrass farms along the Wilson, Franklin, and Granny White pikes. These were the country gentry who owned the wooden-sided station wagons and the antique cabinets filled with silver trophies from local horse shows. Each year they drove across the Old Hickory Boulevard, opened the tail gates of their station wagons, and drank silver cups of Jim Beam to toast the running of the Iroquois Memorial Steeplechase.

I suddenly realized how much Brentwood had changed. The horse farms had been carved into subdivisions for record-company executives whose furniture was trucked in from the West Coast and New York. The local stores catered to the new wealth of the music business, or to the dollars of tourists who daily rode the vans and buses through Brentwood to glimpse the homes of music stars. The local liquor store had the decor of a clubhouse at Churchill Downs, and there are enough track stores to outfit the entire field in the Triple Crown. As songwriter Bob McDill remarked, "The first thing music people do when they hit Brentwood is to buy a few acres and a horse or two." They take their animals to the opulent veterinary clinic in Brentwood. The animal hospital is so luxurious that I suspect poor whites and blacks have it much worse in Mississippi. There is carpeting, piped-in music, half a dozen animal examining rooms, and an elaborate surgery.

When I was a child my best friend lived on a hill above the

village. Brentwood in the 1940s consisted of Noble's cafe, Pew-itt's Garage, a grocery, and the local Methodist church. We would sit on the high slope above his stone house, smoke rabbit tobacco and watch for one of those marvelous, sweptback 1947 Stude-bakers to pass below on the highway. The Studebakers have gone, and so has the house which was moved to make way for another subdivision.

At Brentwood, I drove west along the Old Hickory Boule-vard, which used to be more a back road than a boulevard. Until the great land boom struck Brentwood, Old Hickory was a nar-row two-lane path across the hills and through the bluegrass horse farms. Nashville summers can become blistering, yet the air al-ways seemed cooler on the old pike. Now in the daylight hours the road was jammed with two types of vehicles: the dusty Mercedes and Jags bearing CB antennas—a sure giveaway for a country musician's automobile—and the tour vans and buses, packed with ardent country-music fans who are shipped out daily from Nashville, armed with cameras and cardboard lunch boxes of fried chicken to seek the "homes of the stars."

General Hood's weary army had also gone through Brent-wood. They moved northward on the Franklin Pike, through the fields and the Otter Creek Hills, across the same land where Waylon Jennings, Tammy Wynette, and others live today. Then Hood crossed the Brown's Creek Valley and halted his army on the high ground along Woodmont Boulevard, just north of the elegant mansion where Minnie Pearl now lives. He would wait now for the bluecoats in Nashville to attack.

We were all outcasts that night, these phantoms of the past, myself, and the country-music culture dwelling on the battle-ground. I had returned to the white fences, rock walls, limestone brooks, and the green hills, but I could never again be a part of the straitened Southern fundamentalism which still encompassed the life of the region. I wondered, also, about the musicians and the songwriters who lived among this world of Junior League teas and fund-raising bazaars. The music crowd lived here, but

were they here at all, or were they aliens in a world of old frater-
nity grads from Vanderbilt?

We were not the only Ishmaels on the old field. Hood's barefoot, ragged army was a ghost of the once-mighty force which
had fought at Shiloh, Chickamauga, and Atlanta. The army was
only a fraction of its former size, with its starving horses, ram-
shackle wagons, and worn artillery. I suspect that their Southern
comrades in Nashville viewed the Confederate force as something out of the past, 20,000 followers of a dream which had
perished. Nashville was alive now with new industry and railroads. New names jammed the census rolls, and the old planter
class was gone. Not long after the war, lands were sold off from
Belmont, Traveler's Rest, Belle Meade, and other once-great
plantations. The lush fields were subdivided and then divided
again. Music Row was spawned on the old fields of Belmont,
and Hank Williams lived in gaudy splendor on the lands of
Traveler's Rest.

All of this was happening already in that icy early December
when Hood's shivering army awaited a Union force almost four
times its size. The weather had changed after the Franklin battle,
and the rebels, many of them barefoot, left bloody footprints in
the snow and ice.

I wheeled northward from Old Hickory Boulevard onto the
Granny White Pike. The pike is an ancient road, and was old
even when Andrew Jackson rode back from a Mississippi hon-
eymoon with his bride Rachel. I spent a large part of my life
along this turnpike, and grew up with the aura of the Civil War
that pervades Nashville. The roads which lead off this narrow
pike lined with white fences bear names such as Robert E. Lee
and Beauregard. I passed Eddy Arnold's farm, thinking how I
had once courted his next door neighbor in my 1953 Plymouth,
and drove on through Granny White Gap.

The gap is a cool defile where the road cuts through the Over-
ton Hills. It was summer, and I rolled down the window to
inhale the scent of the honeysuckle which lines the gap. Union

and rebel cavalrymen had battled furiously in this pass during the battle of Nashville which came after a thaw in mid-December. For years I had walked home from school along the pike. I walked even in the snow, which clung to the old rock walls and covered the banks of upper Brown's Creek. Then a thaw would come, the snow would melt, and the rich, dark earth become soggy. That's the way it happened in 1864, and long lines of federal blue drove General Hood's thin ranks back past the homes of Tammy Wynette and Minnie Pearl.

The Confederates were too few to fight and too weak to retreat, so they halted for one last stand. Off to the left of the Granny White Pike, lights glimmered in homes atop Shy's Hill, where country singer Sonny James and other important people from Music Row live. General Hood anchored his left flank on this eminence, waiting for the dreaded assault from the federal troops over on the Hillsboro Road. I grew up near the hill and tramped over it long before the real estate entrepreneurs staked out desirable lots. I still have the brass facing of a pocket watch someone dropped during the battle, a jar of spent bullets, and some fragments of Yankee artillery shells. First the shells had come, and then the Union soldiers had swarmed up the hill. The rebel defenses melted, and the survivors scrambled through the fields toward the Granny White Pike.

My automobile headlights swept against a battlefield marker, and I turned east from the pike along a long rock wall. The wall has been there since the 1850s, and was the northern boundary of an old plantation. I grew up along the old stone wall, which defined the limits of the back lawn of my family home. During the battle, the wall was the fortification of the center of Hood's line, held by old General "Blizzards" Loring. Captured at Vicksburg, Loring was exchanged to fight again when the end came for the western rebels at Nashville.

It was the end. The federals swarmed across the wall and down the Franklin and the Granny White pikes. The Confederate soldiers fought rearguard actions across Oak Hill and Brentwood, but they accomplished nothing. A month later, perhaps 5,000 survivors gathered in Mississippi. The war was over in the West, and soon Robert E. Lee would give up the fight in Virginia.

It was late the night I drove down the lane by the old wall toward my family's home. I glanced at the passing cluster of comfortable houses along the old battleground. Enough outside lights still burned so that a passerby could see them well. It could have been upper-middle-class American gothic anywhere—the spacious two-storied houses with paved driveways, manicured lawns surrounded by white wooden fences, and the two carports for three automobiles. Even the dogs who rummaged through the roadside debris were the large, expensive breeds. Make a few changes and one would have a well-fed suburb of Minneapolis.

But Minneapolis does not have the rock wall, or the silver-colored battle markers that flashed by in my automobile's headlights. The South has never recovered from the disaster at that wall, from Hood's rout at Nashville or Robert E. Lee's surrender in Virginia. Instead, Southerners since Appomattox have lived outside of the American dream of plenty and success, alienated from the basic national myths.

It was five below zero at the Minneapolis airport, and a deep snow covered the parking lot. My host, a local executive, snaked the fancy Mercedes along a narrow path between snowbanks, while the car radio gave us the nasal tones of Tammy Wynette. Almost every year I come to Minnesota to address a dinner of politicians, physicians, and businessmen who are Confederate enthusiasts. They gather at the Northstar Hotel, down some bourbon, and refight the battle of Gettysburg.

The snow came down harder as country crooner Sonny James came on the radio. "God, isn't he great?" the driver asked. He is good, but I wondered why Sonny James was a hero in frozen Minneapolis. Sonny James should be idolized by some Good Ole Boy in Eufala, Alabama, who lives in a mobile home with a wife named Sue Ellen, wears short hair, goes to the local Baptist church, and drives a pickup with a bumper sticker which warns that if you try to take away his gun, he will blow off your god-damn head.

Now the Mercedes radio provided the strains of sultry Barbara Mandrell and one of her good hard-core cheating songs. While the driver kept time on the steering wheel, I blurted out a question which had bothered me for a long time. "Why do you like this kind of music?" I asked. "Why does a Minnesota boy who has never been anywhere in the South except Key West and the Atlanta airport want to listen to Waylon Jennings?" I asked him as well why a group of upper crust Minneapolis people laid out the money to bring up a speaker who wrote books about the Confederacy. Why didn't they bring in some professor who wrote about General Grant?

"Hey," my host responded. "Most of my friends are business executives in Minneapolis. Know what kind of movies we always go to see? We never miss a Burt Reynolds flick about the South— "Gator," "W.W. and the Dixie Dancekings," and all the rest. You people down there have something different, some sort of individualism that we admire."

What intrigued my Northern friend was something more than individualism. It was a Southern mind which reflects a culture set apart from the mainstream of our national faith. When defeat came in 1865, the psychological trauma experienced by Dixie was a God-awful affair. The emotional pain of defeat ranged far beyond the statistics of over a million men killed or maimed, and the billions of dollars which had been lost in the destruction of schools, railroads, banks, and private property. The real shock occurred when Southerners realized that they were living outside the American heritage of success.

When one reads today the wartime editorials of the Richmond newspapers or the letters written from army camps to families back home in Charleston or New Orleans, the immense depth of the belief that God was on the Confederate side is all too evident. When that belief was shattered, the Confederates endured the humiliation of an Appomattox Courthouse and half a dozen other army surrenders. With peace came spiritual depression—the psychological questioning by a land which had discovered that it was outside the Calvinistic theme of success. The Protestant ethic had failed them, and they felt alienated from God and everyone else.

So in the decades after 1865, Southerners groped for some rationale. They ennobled Robert E. Lee as the peerless Southerner, arguing that Lee's Jesus-like character was proof that the righteous do not always prevail. They published small, pitiful magazines, such as *Our Living and Our Dead*, which had articles on how Yankee soldiers were cowards and cheats. Others erected gaudy monuments of Italian marble on Dixie courthouse squares, while their women formed genealogical societies which met to eat rich custards and talked about a war they never knew.

But they did know that Southern life was not in the American mainstream. Some of this was there before the war—several million black slaves, a different rural culture, and the isolation of the planter class. The experience at Hood's rock wall and Appomattox set the South even farther apart, even for people whose ancestors had never owned a slave. The war did not diminish the quality of difference in the Southern mind, but only intensified it. It insured that the South would remain apart from the basic set of American myths.

There was the myth of American abundance. David Potter once wrote a book called *People of Plenty*. He spoke of how the old national faith which shaped our morals, politics, and religion was centered upon our belief that God had blessed us in special ways. We succeeded in the New World because we were caretakers of the Zion in the Wilderness, living symbols of the Calvinistic ideal that reward is an indication of righteousness. After the Civil War, it would have been impossible to convince someone living in the sandhills of Alabama of the truth of this ideal. Long after the guns cooled on Battery Lane, across the old rock wall, the South remained poor, plagued with hookworm, malnutrition, third-rate medical care, and starvation pay for teachers. More important, even before the war there had existed a gnawing sense of economic despair.

Then there was the national doctrine of success—that also went wrong in Dixie. This credo, carried to the New World by the Puritans, preached that achievement is a sign of the bestowal of God's grace. The initial outcome only gave succor to the myth. After all, the Southerner has a deeply imbedded sense of piety— a belief in the established order of doing things—which involves an intense man–God relationship and faith in a life regulated by the Almighty on a daily basis. But where was the Almighty when the one-legged Hood needed him on the battlefield?

This was the beginning of the long anger—the seedbed of much of the modern Southern mind. There is a vital relationship between the mind, the music, and defeat along the old rock wall at Nashville in 1864. There are the dark passions of insecurity seen in the image of the proverbial Good Ole Boy and his music. There is the boastful talk of sex, the display of male bravado in country music, the trappings of Browning shotguns, pickup trucks, and the enthusiasm for Southern college football. The long memory of the war is everywhere in the culture and the music: it shows in the tones of violence and suffering, in the evangelical appeals to Jesus in shabby Alabama churches, in the sense of alienation in being at once Southern and American.

The music is the saga of General Hood and his army failing in the fields outside Nashville. One hears it in Waylon Jennings' album *White Mansions*. The album is a folk opera in which each singer portrays a character who lives through the collapse of the old-plantation order and total defeat of the Civil War. The same message is in Joan Baez's melody of the last days of the Confederacy, and in "The South's Gonna Do It Again," that tale of anger and resolve by the Charlie Daniels Band.

None of them is really about the Civil War, but all are tales of defeat. In the catalogs of country music, songs about the war are almost nonexistent. There are no songs about Robert E. Lee, Jefferson Davis, or Gettysburg. By the same token, other outlets of Southern expression have never addressed the war directly. There is no epic poem of the Confederacy, nor a great novel of the war which transcends the journalism of *Gone with the Wind*. It seems ironic that for a war which remains the central expression of the Southern soul, there are so few mentions of people such as General Hood and his ragtag army on the Nashville battlefield.

Yet the culture is implicitly about nothing else. There is a common thread to a William Faulkner novel, poet Alan Tate's "Ode to the Confederate Dead," and a Waylon Jennings folk opera. The Confederacy is central to all: not battles and generals, but the absolutes of human defeat; the realization that man is both noble and tragic; insecurity, guilt, violence—and above all— alienation.

To begin to understand the Southern soul is to be aware of the importance of what happened to General Hood's army at the rock wall in Nashville. On that first trip home across the bluegrass fields, Will Campbell gave me the message. I drove out the old Knoxville highway to talk with Will Campbell about country music.

Somehow the Creator left the community of Mt. Juliet out of the grand design. The deep hollows of Wilson County lack the broad, rich expanses of Middle Tennessee bluegrass. Much of the soil is in hillside patches strewn with naked layers of limestone rock interspersed with forests of cedar. The paradox of Will Campbell and his heritage begins here in the hollow, twelve miles east of affluent Nashville. His thirty acres off the Knoxville road have little to do with the black earth which for centuries has made Middle Tennessee a Southern Eden.

Even in the Age of Reason, the era of Benjamin Franklin and Thomas Jefferson, Middle Tennessee was Eden. Early travel accounts—mostly oral reports by western Long Hunters—filtered eastward to the Ulster settlers in Virginia and the Carolinas. These were the Scotch–Irish, always a dissatisfied breed who were at once land hungry and land poor. They had always been the noninheritors, who came to the New World in the early 1700s as seven-year indentured servants who worked the Pennsylvania fields to earn their freedom. Once free, ever poor and restless, they moved in the years before the American Revolution, down the Great Appalachian Valley into the Carolinas and Georgia. Will Campbell's people were somewhere in that great migration.

Campbell sat on a bench outside his log hut that he calls his office, in the hollow, long unruly strands of hair clinging to the edges of his balding head. Most Scotch–Irish descendants can boast no coat of arms or elaborate family genealogy, and the lineage of a family becomes more an oral tradition. "My great-great-grandfather was Plez Webb," he remarked softly. "Maybe that was short for Pleasant. I don't know." Campbell toyed with a sharp knife and cedar whittling stick and tried to remember. Maybe the Webbs lived for a time in Georgia, and at some point—perhaps in the great migration—joined up with the Campbells. Eventually the family took root in Will Campbell's birthplace of Amite County, Mississippi. That was years after the Webbs and Campbells had moved down the Great Appalachian Valley.

During the Revolution, the Scotch–Irish were again on the move, as they poured through the Appalachian passes into Tennessee. The trail led eventually along the old Walton Road, across the barren Cumberland Mountain expanse which divided the lush flatlands of the Great Valley from the Eden of Middle Tennessee. They settled along the streams outside Nashville, along the Harpeth and Stone's rivers. Away from the waters, which were bordered by acres of tall canebrake, there were miles of rich land to support Indian corn and to sustain the milch cows, oxen, and swine brought along the old road from Knoxville.

Some thought it was Eden from the very beginning. Sometime in the Paleozoic era, great seas had covered the Nashville area. Billions of shellfish and other creatures were deposited in the ooze of the ancient sea. Then sea after sea came and receded—the last one some 300 million years ago. Meanwhile, a deep layer of limestone sediment was formed from the slow decay of billions of animals and plants. Then the land rose from the sea, in some vast prehistoric eruption which produced a vast limestone dome. Millions of years passed and the dome disappeared into the deep, fertile basin of limestone weathered by the waters around Nashville.

In the Revolutionary War years, the Scotch–Irish newcomers staked out lands by tomahawk and cabin rights in the rich mother earth fields around Nashville. More Ulstermen came after the Revolution, with land warrants for military service. The good lands had diminished in the river bottoms. The newcomers searched out pockets of land in the hollows of the surrounding hills. Some turned into the hollow at Mt. Juliet, off the old pioneer road which had reached Eden from the Great Appalachian Valley.

Preacher Will Campbell lives there now, in the old eighteenth-century log house covered with clapboards. I had never met him, but knew some rudiments of his image. He was the Southern Baptist minister who was nominated for the National Book Award for the poignant story of his Mississippi upbringing, *Brother to a Dragonfly*. I knew that he was considered an outlaw by the institutional forces of the Southern Baptist faith, and that he currently led a small, liberal group of believers called the Committee of Southern Churchmen. Southern religious conservatives had damned him for championing the civil rights cause in the hard years of the 1950s and 1960s when he was a worker in human relations for the National Council of Churches. That was heralded by the liberal establishment until Campbell came to his own long learning in the 1960s. Now God's people were Everyman in Dixie, black and white—even the robed members of the Ku Klux Klan. Campbell had reached for something in the Southern soul that some old comrades in the National Council of Churches could not understand. So he withdrew to the farm in the high ridge country, to edit, write, minister, and sing.

When Campbell came to the hollow in 1963, it was an unwanted place, symbolic of the alienated folk he has championed for almost two decades. The old log house was built at the time the Scotch–Irish pushed across the Walton Road into Middle Tennessee. Later it became a classic hall-and-parlor Southern farmhouse, which in conception had been a "dog-trot" affair of two log pens separated by a breezeway. By the 1960s, the old house was shabby and unwanted. Of the thirty acres of land on which the house sat, only a few could be cultivated; the majority were infested with stony limestone outcroppings and tall, aged cedars. "It was too poor for anything but a subdivision," Campbell said later. By the 1960s, a developer arrived to subdivide the property. Nashville was growing across Stone's River into the hinterlands. A bulldozer was there to level the hall-and-parlor house, while a chainsaw was cranked to fell the huge white oak on the slope above. As Campbell tells the story, the chainsaw erupted with a belch of blue smoke and slashed through the outer layer of bark. "Wait!" the developer shouted. "Maybe someone is fool enough to buy this farm as it is." Years later Marshall Frady would describe Will Campbell as one of God's "divine fools."

Campbell sat on an oak bench outside the log office. Once he traded a mare for the logs, which came from a Kentucky farm not far from the birthplace of Abraham Lincoln. It was a sultry August day and he had come from a patch of corn at the creek bottom to rest. Campbell wiped his bald dome with a red handkerchief and scratched the long strands of hair matted against his gaunt face. "People used to bring theology students down here to look at me," he mused. "They would always say, 'Reverend Campbell'—hell, I hate that term—'we want to observe your life-style because we are in the process of observing alternate styles.' I would tell them I didn't have a life-style. They would always argue with me. 'You live out here on this old farm and plough with a horse, don't you?' That's right, I would say. 'Well, now, you work the land here, write in a log cabin, and wear blue jeans. So don't tell us you don't have a life-style which is intentionally different.' "

Will Campbell pauses to drive the sharp blade of his knife deeper into the soft, cedar whittling stick. "I told them that I moved out here because I did not like subdivisions. I farm to earn a living and because I like to. I don't play golf. I work in a log office because I didn't know how to build a frame house, but I did know how to stack a log or two. And I wear these blue denim shirts and jeans because nobody puts on a Brooks Brothers' suit to work in a field."

Still, his life-style *is* different, and is imbedded in the enigma of the South. Campbell is more than a truck farmer, and the hollow at Mt. Juliet symbolically is more than a farm. Will Campbell is an internationally known religious leader of a church which does not exist. It is a church described by Marshall Frady as "roofless, pulpitless, uncodified, and unpropertied." It is a guerrilla ministry which repudiates the role of institutions—organized churches, governments, and others—in solving human problems.

Will Campbell preaches a faith of existential religious primitivism. He is a revolutionary whose appeal is to an individual testimony which harks back to the Age of Reformation. The revolution—in human rights, poverty, war and peace, and other matters—comes with the human heart. "We are all bastards," Campbell preaches, "but God loves us anyway." God loves us in Campbell's view because "the testimony is there in Second Corinthians, chapter five: 'God was in Christ, reconciling the world unto Himself, no longer holding men's misdeeds against them, and has committed to us this word of reconciliation. Therefore we pray you in Christ's stead, be reconciled.' "

"Be reconciled." Campbell, with his black preacher's hat, wrinkled suit, and walking stick, moves through a mosaic of humanity with this message. In a lecture at Duke University he railed against the institutional church—his own Southern Baptist faith. "Every time a group of Christians have moved from the catacombs to a brush arbor . . . to a wooden-frame building . . . to a brick structure. Each time it has moved, along the way it has lost something. It gave up something it believed about

Jesus and never seemed to get it back." When the Christians moved from the arbor to the steeple-adorned building, the church became an institution—the great enemy which separates rich and poor, blacks and whites in the South. Now the church became emeshed with "bureaucrats, presiding over their altar fires and tea parties in the midst of suffering and death, big spires and steeples costing millions upon millions of dollars and casting their physical shadow upon slums and whores and pimps and addicts and drunks and thieves and rat-infested tenements with the fingers and toes being gnawed off the young and the elderly."

This is not a message that Campbell preaches only within the comfortable confines of a university campus with its aura of free speech. Sometimes he takes the message to the enemy in bold guerrilla thrusts into the heart of the Southern religious establishment. It was the eve of Good Friday at the exclusive St. Paul's Episcopal Church in Richmond where Jefferson Davis and Robert E. Lee had pews during the Civil War. It was here, on a Sunday morning in April 1865, that the message came to the rebel leader that the Confederates must evacuate Richmond. The purple dream of the slaveocracy had vanished; three-and-a-half million blacks would be free although not yet equal, and the South would never be the same.

Campbell began his sermon with a country song, "Good Friday Morning," which was written by a meatcutter in a small Louisiana town. Now it was performed three days before Easter in the elegance of St. Paul's. The song recounted one's failure to be tolerant with others because the values set up by institutions had dimmed the reality. There were "two grown men sitting holding hands," and the singer's prejudice against homosexuals emerged. But then, "I was I was a fool," scorning two men, "one deaf, the other blind." So, Campbell sang, "Here it is Good Friday morning, but for fools like me it's still Thursday night. . . . Lord it's almost Easter Sunday, and I can't even spell salvation right."

Salvation spelled correctly that evening was an attack on the institutional rigors which conflicted with Campbell's primitive

Christianity of redeemed human love. "We're the ones who kill our babies in the womb of their mothers, and put your children in the electric chairs. The U. S. of A? We're the ones who stole this country from some dark-skinned people. Committed genocide to keep it . . . killed them . . . drove them like cattle to keep it . . . bought and sold some more dark-skinned people to build the country . . . fought two global wars to sustain it . . . raped Mexico and the Philippines. Vietnam . . . God, did you forget about that one?"

The core of Campbell's message is a simple union of things spiritual and real. Formal churches with stained glass windows, ornate pews, and social clubs only separate men from God because they divide men from one another. "Jesus is in the streets," Campbell believes. At one meeting in Atlanta, he argued that "We have been so brainwashed, so victimized, so conditioned by the organized, institutionalized churches and we equate the Christian faith with these most evil of all institutions, those high spires, and stained glass, and big bells, and silver chalices, and parking lots, and Betty Crocker kitchens for the sacrament of coffee hours. . . . Now Brothers and Sisters, ain't that a bitch?"

The essence of Campbell's radical ministry was embodied in a conversation at a university campus seminar on religion. A persistent theology professor repeated the same question, over and over: "What is your actual business, Reverend Campbell—I mean, what do you believe in?" Finally Campbell lost his patience and roared, "I have been trying to tell you! I believe in Jesus, goddamit, Jesus! Through the saving grace of His death on the cross, we have all been reconciled to each other. So if we accept this gift, we're free. There ain't no need to hate anyone! Getting the word around about that—that is my business, professor!"

Imagine King David's encampment in the rocky enclaves of the Judean hills. His primitive Israelite bands were still in the stone age of weaponry. Below on the plains of Gaza were the people of the fatted calf—the Philistines with their iron weapons and superior numbers. In this case, the rock-ribbed hollow at

Mt. Juliet is the fortress of another outlaw enclave—outmanned but never outfought. The fertile Middle Tennessee plain and Nashville are the fields of the fatted calf.

The Philistines are not the enemies here. To Will Campbell, the sinners are not Nashville's derelicts who prowl garbage cans for Vodka bottles along lower Broad Street, nor the paunchy, greasy men who operate the coin machines in porno parlors below Fifth Avenue. Nor is the enemy the country-music empire. Here is a vast counterculture which appears far removed from the staunch religious-business ethic which dominates Nashville's affairs. Campbell understands the heart of country music, which is the message of General Hood's army defeated on the Nashville field. It is a music with a raw, tough appraisal of life explained in terms of alcoholism, adultery, and violence, but tinged always with the themes of defeat and alienation. Some of the singers have reaped fortunes and live in the finer suburbs. Thousands more—singers, musicians, and writers—have never attained success. They exist in a fringe world void of roots, far from the verities of family and community. Their life is a hazy, seemingly drifting experience, a patchwork of cheap rooming houses in the old Belmont section, shabby motel rooms out along the old Louisville highway, songs delivered for loose change in grimy bars along Broad Street, unpaid bills and constant changes of address; and, finally, for most, pawned musical instruments resting forlornly in shops near Fourth Avenue.

"These people are the poets," Will Campbell insists, and ministers to them, great and small. Some of his friends are national figures—singers such as Waylon Jennings and Kris Kristofferson, or powerful music publishers and songwriters. Most, however, are members of the larger fringe. They are "sidemen" who play in country bands, studio musicians who eke out a living by recording in all-night sessions, has-been performers, hopeful youths searching for discovery, and an array of hangers-on and drifters. Campbell answers their telephone calls in the early morning hours or counsels them in the old log office. Sometimes he marries them, baptizes their children, or preaches funeral rites for their kinsmen.

Will Campbell thrust a wad of chewing tobacco into his right cheek and uttered a brief chuckle. "One of Waylon's boys—plays in his band—came out here one day and said he wanted me to perform his marriage ceremony. But then he said they wanted to get married in the Exit-Inn, over on Elliston Place. I had some doubts about this and at first refused. 'Why not?' the fellow asked. Because, the Exit-Inn is a bar, a country music picking place. Now I've married people in all kinds of places—out in cornfields, beside fishponds, and Lord knows where else. But that looked to me like showmanship. To come to some bar after this boy's band had played there—that looked like showmanship."

Then Campbell paused and gave a wry smile. "You know," he murmured, "he said to me, 'Reverend Campbell, I don't have a regular church. I want to get married at the Exit-Inn because I met my girl there, and because most of my friends are going to be there to watch us play that night. They're folks who stood by me in some hard times, and I want them to be there on a happy night.' "

"Now I get what you're saying," Campbell answered. "You're telling me that that place is *your* church! Well, hell, that's different. I'll do the wedding ceremony."

The *real* enemy, in the eyes of Will Campbell, would have never understood that conversation. To Preacher Will, the foe is the massive organized religious complex of Dixie, which is headquartered in nearby Nashville. This is no city *with* churches. Even for a Southern community where religious fundamentalism is part of the cultural fabric, Nashville is an extreme. Religion is business. During the 1970s almost twenty percent of the city's total manufacturing payroll came from religious publications. During that same era, some forty-two percent of Nashville's property enjoyed a tax-exempt status on religious grounds.

The institutional power of Nashville's religion is overwhelming. Here is the nation's largest religious printing plant (United Methodist Church); the world's largest religious publishing outlet (Baptist Sunday School Board); and the nation's largest publisher and distributor of Bibles. In fact, six religious denominations maintain publishing facilities here which serve half of the Protestant churches in the United States. Over a dozen seminaries and colleges train preachers, missionaries, and laymen to preach and protect the fundamentalist creed. Nashville's reputation as the cultural "Athens of the South"—the home of many academic learning centers—is tied closely to Southern religion. Even the celebrated apex of the city's academic world, Vanderbilt University, had close ties with the United Methodist Church until early in the twentieth century.

Hundreds of acres of Davidson County soil are the domain of conservative colleges and religious academies. David Lipscomb College is the fortress of the ultra-conservative Church of Christ. Although it possesses no central organization and practices congregational autonomy, the Church of Christ has grown since the Second World War into one of the larger Protestant denominations. Though some of its beliefs—baptism by immersion only and absolute Biblical literalism—smack of the primitivism associated with rough-hewn frontier religion, in Nashville, the Church of Christ is a middle-class establishment. Acres of asphalt church parking lots, 110 separate congregations, scores of buses, multimillion-dollar church buildings, television and radio, and local political power—all rest in this body.

But even the power of the Church of Christ is overshadowed by the might of the Southern Baptists in Nashville. If Will Campbell has an enemy, it is in many ways the heritage of his own faith. The Southern Baptist Convention is more than a religion. It is a supercorporation boasting more than thirteen million members nationwide. In eight Southern states, fifty percent of the total religious membership is Baptist, and in five others, the church claims at least forty percent of the total population of churchmen. In fact, the Southern Baptist Convention, which has its headquarters in Will Campbell's Nashville, is larger in assets, revenues, and numbers of staff members than some transnational corporations headquartered in the South. In 1975, the church's assets totaled six billion dollars, compared to a smaller 1.7 billion reported by the Coca-Cola Company. Annual proceeds from revenues reached 1.5 billion dollars. That same year, the Baptist establishment employed more people than were working for the Dow Chemical Corporation or the Coca-Cola Company. Says Will Campbell of this vast institution of his own mother church: "Institutions create the illusion that doing is being, and eventually become only instruments of their own self-perpetuation." Ornate buildings and church basketball teams represent something foreign to Campbell's primitive Christian faith. "All over this country," he remarked, "you have those heroic church steeples casting splendid shadows over people living in misery."

Sometimes Will Davis Campbell, ordained a Baptist minister as a youth, emerges from the hollow at Mt. Juliet to do battle with the Philistines on the Nashville plain. There was the incident in 1968, during the era of civil rights protests and demonstrations against the war in Vietnam. The Southern Baptist leadership decided to install new security measures in one of their major Nashville buildings. Employees were issued punch cards which would admit them to the facility, and a tear gas system was installed to guard against intruders. At the time, Campbell was director of the liberal Committee of Southern Churchmen. In the group's journal, *Katallagete—Be Reconciled*, he described the preventive tear gas system and remarked, "It is all quite human. The Coat of Christ is protected. The tracts and quarterlies and pretty Sunday school cards bearing the good news of Christ crucified and resurrected are damaged only by a little vomit. But since rioters have seldom much to eat the damage will be slight." But do not pity the rioters, Campbell concluded. Instead lament "the plight of the holder of the IBM card, which includes most of us in one form or another." Campbell ended glumly by noting that "*We* are the prisoners of the technological concentration camp of our own doing. . . ."

Soon a well-dressed church executive came to the Mt. Juliet farm. "He took rather robust umbrage at my comments," Campbell said. The two sat in the log office. Campbell attacked a piece of cedar wood with his pocketknife. Occasionally he paused to spit tobacco juice into the sandbox by the large cast-iron wood stove. He listened while the delegate explained that the tear gas system was installed to protect the building against "undesirables." Campbell snorted. "Tell me, for the love of Jesus Christ, exactly who our Lord asked us to serve?" The official tried to explain that there had been "some stealing" on the premises. "Stealing?" Campbell fired back. "Didn't the Lord tell us that if someone steals our coats, give him our cloak also?"

Campbell's voice rose as did his anger. "God help us. We have ended up where our Savior's church regards as *undesirables* those very people it was commanded to save, and to build barricades against them, even if it takes tear gas to do it!"

By then the churchman had begun to sweat, and intoned, "Now, we might be getting a little overzealous here." "No we ain't," Campbell retorted. "We are *supposed* to be zealous. Oh, I'm not blaming *you*," he continued. "You have all that expensive equipment over there and want to protect it. You have to act according to Caesar's terms. But those ain't exactly the gospel's terms, are they?"

They were not always the gospel's terms for Will Campbell, either. Here was the beginning of the paradox which involves Campbell and the mind of his South. There is little in Campbell or his heritage which appears consistent to an outside observer. He is the epitome of the Southern enigma—a maze of apparent contradictions.

Once he was a seventeen-year-old fledgling Baptist preacher, ordained in a small Mississippi church. Now he fights against the structure of his fundamentalist Baptist heritage. His Deep South Baptist tradition demanded obedience to church authority, noninvolvement in social matters such as labor problems and race relations, and intense supra-loyalty to God and country. Instead, Campbell preached a revolutionary message which would dismantle the institutional church. He had marched in labor disputes and racial demonstrations, fought against abortion and capital punishment, and cried out against the war in Vietnam. His Southern Baptist brethren adhere to a rigid moralistic code. From the pulpit, Campbell occasionally sprinkles his sermons with profanity born of a rich Mississippi vocabulary. Meanwhile, he carries along a bottle of bourbon in the battered suitcase when he ministers to black militants, condemned prisoners, members of the Ku Klux Klan, and a host of others.

But first would come the beginnings of a long changing, and Will Campbell's own realization of the soul of the South. It began in rural, Depression-ridden Amite County, Mississippi, on his father's small, poverty-stricken cotton farm. At first Campbell was in step with the habits of an aspiring rural Southern Baptist preacher. But somehow even in that early time he was different. When his kinsmen finished school, they attended a small, nearby Mississippi junior college. Will Campbell broke with his roots in a modest way, and attended a Baptist college in Louisiana. It was the beginning of a new awareness in his life, something which was deepened with the Second World War. Campbell set aside his minister's deferment and volunteered for duty in the South Pacific.

Then came New Caledonia, Saipan, Guam, and Tinian, where his unit watched the B-29 squadron leave to drop the atomic bomb on Japan. It was the dawn of an awareness of racial injustice. Then came the reading of Howard Fast's novel, *Freedom Road*. "That one book, I suppose, did more to kind of turn my head around where race was concerned," Campbell remembered. The war ended, and Campbell was educated on the G.I. bill at Wake Forest College, Tulane University, and eventually took a degree from the Yale University Divinity School. Then he returned home.

He was home, but not really. Slowly, he would become Will Campbell the social activist, reviled even by some of his own kin in East Fork, Mississippi. His career as a Baptist minister spans less than a meager two years, when he preached for a small Louisiana church. Something was wrong, even then, with Will Campbell's sermons. They spoke of problems in workers' rights, the danger of right-wing politics in the national government, and other unsettling topics. One woman parishioner complained, "One Sunday you preach about McCarthy and the next about negroes." Or about labor problems.

Elizabeth was a community two hundred miles away, the air rancid with the odor of the local paper mill and the streets displayed dismal wooden row houses. When workers sought to organize a union, Preacher Will Campbell appeared on the streets. He walked the picket line, drank coffee and bourbon in long night sessions, and addressed the mill employees. Sometimes he did other things that never suited the image of a small-town Southern Baptist preacher. He drove over to visit friends at the all-black Grambling College. He also paid the black woman who did his wash the minimum wage. "Don't do that. You'll ruin the help. All of our maids will want that," someone cautioned.

It was time to leave. "I knew by then," he recalls, "that I could never be a minister in the formal sense. My nervous system couldn't take it. The principles of Jesus were the same, but there had to be another way to approach the problem. Do it by example, not by preaching. Hell, who pays attention to a pulpit sermon anyway?"

Will Campbell plucked an ear of corn from the truck (small) garden in the creek bottom and adjusted his battered straw hat. "My going to Ole Miss had nothing to do with race relations. I went there to spend the rest of my life. My folks lived in Amite County and my brother Joe was living in Meridian and we were extremely close. I didn't want to be a big gun in the Southern Baptist Convention. Besides, I wasn't a red-hot crusader on race or anything else."

But he did become a crusader, probably because of a mixture of belief and circumstance. In the 1950s and early 1960s, Will Campbell became a prominent white face amid the sea of black voices demanding equality. He was at Little Rock, Arkansas, escorting black children to a school barricaded by National Guard troops. He was the only white face in the group in Atlanta that fateful day when the Southern Christian Leadership Conference was organized. When demonstrations erupted in Albany, Georgia, Campbell was there, and in Birmingham and elsewhere to negotiate with white business leaders about the rights of black souls. It seemed a long way from Klan-ridden Amite County to the friendship and counsel of Martin Luther King, Jr., Andrew Young, Stokeley Carmichael, and even "Rap" Brown.

Then came another long changing in the 1960s. Will Campbell would never return home to Amite County. So now he lives on the farm at Mt. Juliet and ministers to all he considers to be the downtrodden.

Several years ago a Southern critic and author, John Egerton, wrote an article called "What Does Will Campbell Do in a Year?" Reluctantly, Campbell had agreed to allow Egerton access to his appointment book, which told nothing of the private hours of anguish spent with the downtrodden ones, but displayed only a hodgepodge of public appearances. The restless, guitar-laden Campbell seemed to be always on the road. For example, in October one year he attended a symposium on the South at a Mississippi university. Then there were two days of meetings in an effort to block extradition to Pennsylvania of a prison escapee who had been living a quiet, law-abiding life in a community there. Then came a retreat for East Tennessee Episcopal priests, followed by meetings with leaders of the Southern Prison Ministry, a special interest of Campbell's. Then came a human relations seminar in Atlanta, a lecture to a class at the Vanderbilt University Divinity School, and much private counsel for some attorneys, corporate executives, and other lost souls.

November was little different. Campbell drove to the maximum security Brushy Mountain State Prison in Tennessee to speak with inmates about creative writing. Then he flew across the Blue Ridge Mountains to a North Carolina college for a session on black studies. Campbell returned to the hollow at Mt. Juliet to perform a wedding for someone in the country-music trade; shortly after, Studs Terkel came to stay at the guest house. Then came a speech at Florida State University.

Through the winter, the chronicle was similar. The wandering preacher in the wide black hat clutched his battered guitar case and roamed about in search of converts to his guerrilla Christianity. There were appearances on the Dick Cavett television show, a religious retreat in Mississippi, and a retreat of Lutheran campus ministers in southern Georgia. Then a young woman arrived at the guest quarters on the hill—the aged Dolan house. She had been told that her cancer was incurable and simply wanted to be with Will Campbell and his wife Brenda for some days. Later there was a lecture at fashionable Sweetbriar College in Virginia, a wedding performed for a young woman Will had first met in a Georgia jail, a speech in Milwaukee to an ecumenical group involved in inner-city ministry. Then, in Phoenix, Arizona, he would attend a conference of people who had abandoned the faith—dropout priests, nuns, and ministers. And there were visits with friends such as Walker Percy and Jules Feiffer, an ordination sermon for a woman entering the United Church of Christ ministry in Indiana, attendance at the National Conference of Black Churchmen in Atlanta, speaking engagements at Gettysburg College in Pennsylvania and several Southern colleges. Meanwhile, the telephone kept ringing in the log office. An airline stewardess and a Cherokee Indian wanted Campbell to perform their marriage ceremony; later he baptized them in the fish pool outside of the office. Then there was a call from a church leader in Norway who wanted to discuss an upcoming conference on social activism, a local farm neighbor whose son was dying of cancer, a well-known country-music singer, a Ku Klux Klan leader in the Carolinas who just wanted to talk to Brother Will.

Through all this activity he remains just that: Brother Will Campbell, whose life embodies the essential paradox of the South. Ask him what he does and he will answer in simple terms: "I am just a preacher."

MORNING

William the gardener always seemed ageless, as he forked the black, pungent Nashville earth. "How old is William?" children asked their elders. "You can't tell with colored people," they answered. "No one knows how old a colored person is."

A child of the 1940s was not expected to grasp the subtle distinctions of language when one spoke of black people. Children were told that William was "colored" and that his residential area of South Nashville was "the colored section." This made perfectly good sense. After all, it was endorsed by the city's bus service, the Southern Coach lines. Each day William, clad in bib-overalls and flannel shirt, rode out through the old Nashville battlefield in the style of royalty. The bus company had seen to his special treatment. It allotted him a special section emblazoned with the sign THIS SECTION RESERVED FOR COLORED PATRONS ONLY. The paradox again: courtesy and contempt, "patrons" who were inferiors.

To white people, William the gardener was something else. Certainly the older generation never referred to a black person as a "nigger" or used fouler terms such as "coon" or "jigaboo." Careful, paternalistic use of language was a mark of the rising middle-class Nashville culture of the 1940s. Only the blue-collar element which lived in North Nashville or across the Cumberland River in the old Edgefield district, now known as East Nashville, would use such distasteful terms. Instead, to the adults he was "nigra William," who lived in a black section known as South Nashville. By the 1940s, South Nashville was running over with a black population confined between the aging Broad Street business district and the surrounding world of white suburban neighborhoods. Each workday morning the women boarded city buses bearing names such as "Belmont," "Granny White Pike," or "South Eighth–Franklin" to serve as maids for white housewives. Some of their husbands—like William—came along as gardeners. His full name was William Goldthwaite. A century ago, his father, a slave in Montgomery, Alabama, had been owned and named by a merchant who bestowed the last name. William worked for families who lived in the Melrose area, along General Hood's first line of defense at the battle of Nashville.

William would appear in the early morning, always carrying that mysterious brown paper bag or shopping bag that all black workers carried into Melrose. The children were too young to understand its survival function for William and the others, unaware that the bag held precious bits of cast-off food and clothing discarded by the white suburban women.

There were some well-defined images which children would remember. They followed William constantly as he labored in the Nashville earth. At noon, after a family had dined, William was allowed to enter the kitchen. There, amid the scents of sweat, tobacco juice, and soil, William now could eat. Always he entered by the back door, and would return to his yard duties. Much of the time he sang, usually old white Protestant hymns, such as "Jesus Keep Me Near the Cross" or black spirituals, such as "Swing Low, Sweet Chariot." "Those nigras like to sing," our elders would comment. "They are just like children."

So he told a child's story, not once but scores of times in the humid Nashville heat of July. The black stubble of his beard was even then beginning to whiten, and there was the closeness of appearance to an Uncle Remus stereotype. Sometimes he told us the tales in the shade of a maple tree. Always the stories were from the characters of Joel Chandler Harris, of the wily B'rer Rabbit and the cunning of B'rer Fox. The children did not understand something which author Harris admitted, a point which has been underscored in recent years by Southern essayist Louis D. Rubin, Jr., in a thoughtful article entitled "Uncle Remus and the Ubiquitous Rabbit." The rabbit was the black man, and in folklore, a hero symbol who used weakness and cunning to overcome helplessness.

Nashville's white population in the 1940s did not consider William to be helpless at all. Even in the center of New Testament fundamentalism, with its emphasis on the teachings of Jesus, everything was separate and not equal—separate schools and neighborhoods, eating places, and drinking fountains. Always there was the fear that black people would become "uppity." By the early 1950s, not long before Will Campbell arrived in Nashville, those fears began to take the shape of reality. The city could no longer hold back the restive ambitions of the growing black population which had glimpsed a semblance of equality in the social upheaval of the Second World War. Residential patterns began to shift abruptly as the city grew rapidly and the black region of South Nashville broke out of its bounds as if a dam had collapsed. Blacks began moving into adjacent white blue-collar districts, while small businessmen and urban developers claimed the old region of South Nashville. In turn, the white laboring class began to flee southward, into the old Melrose district, into the realm of the Nashville middle-class.

In the early 1950s, the streets of Melrose were lined with the signs of houses for sale. Like Hood's army, people were retreating from the first Confederate battle line through Melrose in 1864. This time the enemy was black. The retreat halted precisely where General Hood had reined in that day over a century ago to form a new battle line. Oak Hill was a solid upper-middle-class area stretching to the hills south of Nashville, and was bounded on the north by the old rock wall.

William the gardener followed, like one of those stereotype black servants culled from a romantic Southern novel. He worked the dark, rich limestone soil. Sometimes his strong hands raised the spade from the yielding ground, exposing chalk-white lead bullets and fragments of artillery shells crusted with dark brown rust. Nearby always was the limestone rock wall which slaves, such as William's father, had built in the years before the Civil War. "Smell this land," William would tell the children, as he thrust the spade deeper, uncovering flecks of limestone.

But the winds which blew against the old rock wall had changed by the 1960s. William was older, with white stubble on his jowls. And he worked silently, no longer singing the old songs in a melodious voice. The older generation diagnosed the situation: "William is not happy anymore. All of this civil rights agitation has upset him." They did not understand that B'rer Rabbit was dead, buried somewhere out in the dark earth where "nigra" William had toiled for some quarter of a century for my family. William had said enough words over the animal for years, and now left him in the bluegrass soil, while he grasped for something else. Now William wanted to talk about an upstart Baptist preacher in Alabama named Martin Luther King.

Sometimes in those last days William did not have his facts quite in order. Recounting how the Union army invaded the Alabama of his slave-father, William described their rows of machine guns. And his estimation of Abraham Lincoln did, in truth, include the plaudit that Lincoln was smarter than the others in his day because he had attended the electoral college.

But his directions were right, even if the facts went astray in those last conversations beside the old wall. William was not "upset," as the whites thought. He was venting decades of black anger and awareness, a culmination of years of humiliation which had been buried beneath mother earth, or at least hidden in appearance. Now it all came out of the earth, fresh with the winds which surged across the old rock wall, just as General George Thomas's bluecoats had streamed against the thin rebel lines: all the long hours on the back seat of the Nashville bus with its reserved section, the days of the brown paper bag, and the hungry hours of waiting outside the back door for his noon meal.

William was both the storyteller and the tale, a constant reminder of the contradictions of the South. They were there every day when he left work and rode the bus homeward through the old Belmont district. En route, the road curved around a tall hill where the once-elegant Belmont mansion, built by Adelicia Acklen, sat. Now modern buildings surrounded the house, which has been incorporated into the Southern Baptist Belmont College.

According to local tradition, Adelicia Hayes Franklin Acklen Cheatham remarked later that she had married three times: for money, for love, and for social prominence. The money came to her as a young woman before the Civil War, when Adelicia Hayes married Issac Franklin, the wealthiest slave trader in the South. Franklin did not live many years and she became the mistress of several plantations in Louisiana and Tennessee, with mansions financed by the toil of thousands of black men and women whom Issac Franklin had sold into the cotton and sugar lands of the Deep South. Later she married a wealthy Alabama planter named Joseph Acklen, and the two built Belmont mansion. It was perhaps one of the most elegant homes in Dixie, filled with expensive furnishings purchased in Europe, and with gardens which extended for several modern city blocks, an apiary, and a bear house.

The bear house and the ornate wrought-iron decor were paid for by Acklen's chattels in Alabama, where William the gardener's father was a slave. It is not difficult to envision William sitting on the Belmont bus, overalls grimed with sweat and dirt, clutching his precious bag as the vehicle rounded the curve alongside the old mansion gardens. They are both dead now, specters which rise up in memory to affirm the paradox of Southern life. There was Adelicia Acklen, in the twilight of Belmont's glory in the years after Appomattox. She married again, this time to a prominent local physician. The lavish ceremony, which cost ten thousand Yankee dollars, took place in the vast gardens, designed by Issac Franklin, her first husband. He had purchased humans by the thousands at cheap prices from the dwindling tobacco empire on the Atlantic coast, and sold them to the new, rich cotton planters of the Mississippi delta.

They were carried to Will Campbell's land, down the dark Indian path known as the Natchez Trace into central and southern Mississippi. Along the way, they rested for the night by streams such as the Buffalo River. Sometimes they uttered Jesus sounds—long, high-pitched chants of defeat and resolution, born in the work-gang songs of the tobacco lands of the upper South.

They would also be Will Campbell's Jesus sounds, first heard at the Glory Hole. The crystal waters of the east fork of the Amite River slowed in a long, sluggish bend to form a baptismal pool. Already months before, in the spring, Will Davis Campbell, age seven, hesitated before walking down the narrow aisle of the tiny East Fork Baptist Church. "Go ahead," his protective older brother had said, as he nudged the small, frail boy into the aisle. The congregation sang "Just As I Am, Without One Plea," and Campbell finally moved forward. The young preacher, not yet a graduate of a backwater Louisiana Baptist school, intoned, "Will Davis Campbell, do you repent of your sins and wish to follow Jesus Christ in Baptism?" The boy nodded, and then the vote was taken among the members sitting on the hard, oak pews. It was Will Campbell's time for salvation.

But it was yet too cold at the Glory Hole. Even the cotton lands of southwest Mississippi were suffering the bleak winds of a blackberry winter. Real salvation would wait for June 1931.

Two years into the Great Depression, the Campbell family, like others in Amite County, was reduced to gnawing poverty. Six bales of cotton, sold that year at four cents a pound, brought little. Somehow the father, Lee Campbell, found the money. The mail order went to Sears-Roebuck for new baptismal clothing—white linen pants and a white shirt. The package did not arrive in time for the ceremony. Will Campbell found his Lord on the clay river bank clad in an old summer suit. On the bluff above the stream, the small congregation, mostly relatives and all small

cotton patch farmers, watched as the fledgling preacher pushed
Will Campbell beneath the waters. Then they sang his first Jesus
sounds, the old camp-meeting hymn, "Happy Day, Happy Day,
When Jesus Washed My Sins Away."

The waters of the east fork flowed across Amite County, where
the drab sandy clay and pine belts of Central Mississippi merged
with the fertile delta soil which extended to the big river at points
such as Vicksburg and Fort Adams. Sometimes when Will
Campbell rode twelve miles with his father in the wagon to the
county seat at Liberty, he saw the courthouse which was built
twenty years before the Civil War began at Fort Sumter.

Liberty was part of that long memory of defeat, of the human
travail of slavery and the aftermath of the Confederate surrender.
Campbell's great-grandfather, Plez Webb, had come here in the
Great Migration even before Mississippi became a state in 1817.
Then the river country was still raw territory, filling with slaves
and huge fields of cotton. When Plez Campbell arrived in 1816,
Amite County boasted 3,365 white settlers and 1,694 slaves.
Water mills powered huge gins on the Amite River. The inven-
tion of the cotton gin had increased the demand for black bonds-
men. They came by the thousands from the older South, from
Virginia and the Carolinas, or from the upcountry of Kentucky
and Tennessee. Some, we have seen, were led in long trains down
the Natchez Trace. Others were pushed across the new territo-
rial road which had opened through the farmlands of central Alabama. Many came to Liberty, just on the verge of the great delta
plantation empire, to be put on the auction block just north of
the courthouse in Liberty. By 1830, a good field hand, strong
and with promise of bearing offspring, could bring fifteen
hundred dollars. Liberty meant slavery.

Sometimes Will Campbell takes down his guitar and strums a
melody he wrote called "Hello, Brother Mother, Friend of Mine."
Brother Mother was a twelve-year-old black field hand. Will's
father's heart condition kept him from hard farm labor. Strong
Leon was paid five dollars a month to work on the Campbell
place. Leon never saw the cash. The wages were given to his

father in hog meat and eggs. The boy slept in the smokehouse
and worked in the fields with Will. Often they played with
knives, wrestled or jostled each other with pet nicknames such
as "Brother Mother." They were too young to know that age in
Amite County would bring a chasm between them.

The black youth's ancestors had worked to build and sustain
the Greek Revival mansions in Liberty. Sometimes Will Campbell saw them, only from the outside, when his father had business at the county seat. They were part of Campbell's own sense
of time and place in Amite County—that blending of tradition,
race, family, and the memory of the Civil War. There was the
lavish Skinner house three blocks south of the courthouse. Slaves
had carved the elaborate mantel and five of them died when the
master's steam sawmill exploded. The Talberts' were new rich
people who had migrated to southwest Mississippi during the
rising era of the cotton kingdom. Most of the migrants failed to
make a fortune in the delta earth. Plez Webb, Will Campbell's
grandfather, was a yeoman like most Amite settlers. Meanwhile,
the Talberts' owned slaves who made bricks and built the mansion. Another house slave with artistic skills burned figures of
animals and other objects in the stained pine of the second-floor
ceilings.

The purple dream of a slave empire collapsed in Amite County
after Appomattox, as elsewhere across the lower South. But the
memory of defeat, the awareness of a paradoxical existence of
being both Southern and American only grew. In Liberty, the
memory was enshrined in the Italian marble shaft, twenty feet
high, on the courthouse lawn. After the Confederate surrender,
Mississippi was enmeshed in the dismal poverty and sheer physical agony of war's aftermath. In 1866, one sixth of the state's
entire revenue went to pay for artificial limbs for disabled soldiers. Still, the Amite people somehow accumulated the huge
sum of $3,322 and sent to New Orleans for the monument. The
stonemasons chiseled on the face the names of all the Confederates who perished in the war, and then sent it upriver by boat.
Then the shaft was hauled the last thirty miles of the journey

across dirt roads to Liberty. On the face is the marble wreath, which surrounds the motto AT REST.

The memory of war was not at rest in Liberty, certainly not twelve miles away in the poverty of the East Fork community. Here, too, was part of Will Campbell's sense of place—the awareness of the Southern contradictions of success and failure, black and white, American and Mississippian.

Home first was the "Old Place," where Lee Campbell had taken his bride when she was scarcely seventeen. "There was no electricity, no running water, no telephone," Campbell remembered later. "My daddy had not been in the World War and so he didn't get a pension like a lot of my uncles and cousins who lived around us in the community. It was a strange feeling of alienation I had as a kid, even from my own kind. Not that we had less, but our daddy was not a veteran, so the neighbors had more.

"At least the neighbors had drinking water. The well never worked at the Old Place, so daddy hauled two buckets of water at a time from Grandpa Bunt's place."

Grandpa Bunt was John Edward Campbell, who revealed for his grandson the absolute paradoxes of the Southern existence. There were all the family tales, the rich oral tradition which had become imbedded in Southern music. As a boy, Will heard the old man talk of his hatred for violence. Yet when his own children had been young, Grandpa Bunt had hitched a wagon and carried his five boys to Liberty to witness the hanging of a young man who had murdered two kinsmen.

"Why did he do it?" Will Campbell mused. "He was a Stoic, like a lot of old Southerners were, particularly before the Civil War. Basically he said 'The world should not be this way but it is.' You know, he was no stranger to tragedy. He lost most of his children when he was in his middle twenties. They died of the bleeding flux. He built the coffins, then carried each one on his shoulder out to the burying ground."

Sometimes the old man sat with Will and his brother Joe in the barn and told stories of the Civil War. His father had fought in the first great battle at Shiloh, just north of the Mississippi border. Tall, moustached General Albert Sidney Johnston was the great hope of the Confederacy in early 1862. From the railroad town of Corinth, he marched a ragged army of Confederates, many in Mississippi regiments, along roads mired with mud to attack the federals at a steamboat dock called Pittsburg Landing. A new officer named Ulysses Grant was taken by surprise as the rebel yell shrieked through the bottomlands along the Tennessee River. Sidney Johnston rode too far in the advance and a Yankee minie ball clipped an artery in his leg. He bled to death, although simple modern first aid could have saved him, just as a single medical injection could have saved the children of Grandpa Bunt from the bleeding flux. Grandpa Bunt's father was scarcely more fortunate than the General. Wounded in battle, he returned home to die at the old home place in Amite County. There was no undertaker available, because all were with their embalming wagons on the Shiloh battlefield. Instead, the soldier was placed in a wooden coffin by the front door, so that the chill, early April breezes would slow decomposition until the circuit-riding preacher arrived to preach the burial service.

It was all part of a closely woven Southern culture of family, school, and church. "Everything was intermingled," Campbell remembers. "Family blended into school, and school into church. Everybody attended the East Fork school. And when someone in the community died, they suspended school. Everyone, first through twelfth grade, were marched over to the Baptist church for the funeral. We thought nothing of it. It was just part of life. . . ."

Life and death was a sense of time and place, of the constants of the past and present. There was a Stoic reality of nonchange, a classical acceptance that life is at best a success and a failure. "I don't remember that a word like 'happy' was even in our vocabulary," Campbell said later. "Certainly there was happiness, and unhappiness, but nobody thought about it that way."

The New South was late in coming to backwater rural Mississippi, but arrived during the early years of the Great Depression. Already, in the years of the First World War, gangs of huge, sweaty black men armed with crosscut saws had come to Moore's pasture, the favorite retreat for Will Campbell and his brother Joe. They hewed and dragged away the great pine forest which in a nearby sawmill would be transformed into boards for army barracks or ship decks. Later, in the 1930s, the Hattiesburg Hercules Company returned to rip out the pine stumps that were rich in resin needed for precious naval stores.

Then came the high lines of the Tennessee Valley Authority, stretching away from the big dam at Muscle Shoals, Alabama. Brother Joe eventually went off to work at the Civilian Conservation Corps camp at Brookhaven. The WPA came through Amite County and constructed a new, sleek, twenty-seat wooden privy at the East Fork school.

"I never understood why that outhouse didn't fall into a hole in the ground," Campbell recalled. "They dug this big trench, over twenty feet long, and built the frame privy around it. Something had to hold the building up. One day I slipped into the outhouse during recess with a kitchen match. Of course we did not have toilet paper then—just newspapers or pieces of a Sears-Roebuck catalog. I lit a piece of paper and dropped it down the hole. The entire bottom of the pit lit up in flames and I realized suddenly that it was full of paper. I ran back to the schoolroom, expecting that privy to go up in smoke. I waited for hours before I realized it didn't burn."

It could not burn, because already Will Campbell was a relief child in the new Roosevelt programs which had constructed the privy. When Campbell was scarcely more than an infant, Lee Campbell moved his family. "Moving" to a Southerner wedded to the ties of family and community was then a relative term. The family took their few belongings and trudged several hundred yards to another house where there was water. "For a long time my daddy thought he was well off," Campbell recalled. "Hell, he could walk out on the back porch and draw a bucket of water anytime he wished. It was better than times in the Old Place nearby, when we collected water running off the tin roof to drink."

The new house had a bored well, but four cents a pound for cotton did little to help Lee Campbell's offspring in the Depression years. Reluctantly he applied to a federal relief program. The cash vouchers for family necessities did not come. Instead, the government food commodity program gave them fatback, powdered milk, and dried beans.

It was enough to provide lunches at the East Fork school. Will Campbell and his brother first carried their noon meal in small, tin, lard buckets, filled with fried ham, corn bread, and small jars of sorghum molasses. His middle-class schoolmates brought the same fare in paper bags, while the richer children could afford sandwiches of white bread and baloney. "The lard bucket people always sat together," Campbell recalled. "It was something of a small but rather distinct dividing line within a very close society."

He knew, but did not know, that the institutionalized rigors of society were beginning to affect him. The Works Progress Administration erected a new lunchroom at the East Fork school, and federal relief programs allowed a student to have a hot lunch each day for four cents. Three dollars and twenty cents a month for the meals was too much for the Campbell family. "We were in another category," Campbell mused. "The government allowed that those on direct federal relief would be given free lunches. I even remember the name of the lunchroom manager— Mrs. Mrytis Cruise. Every day she took a head count of those to be served by the four-cent hot meal program. Then she would blare out, 'Alright, now all of you little relief children, you hold up your hands.' My fourth-grade sweetheart, someone named Evie Lee—you know, all Southern girls have good double names—she was a four-cent person while I was on relief. I would watch and pray that she wouldn't look at me when we relief children held up our hands. Sometimes I would barely stick up one finger."

It was part of a long beginning of puzzlement, later to become outrage, that institutions—state and church—pulled people apart from themselves, their kin, and other races. More than from the lunchroom incident, the puzzlement increased when a technician from the State Health Department arrived at East Fork to discuss the program for hookworm. The paradoxical land of Mississippi, lush and tepid, blessed with William Faulkner and cursed with the white robes of the Ku Klux Klan, rich in the oral tradition and illiterate, was troubled by the festering malady. The young, nervous health administrator took the boys at East Fork aside and presented each with a small tin receptacle, which looked like a box. "You must take a specimen," he insisted. "What is a specimen?" someone asked. The health official turned nervously to the principal, who cleared his throat. "Well, boys, a specimen is . . . a specimen . . . a small amount of something."

Within hours Will Campbell, brother Joe, and their friends had withdrawn to Moore's pasture to plot their strategy. "By now we knew the federal government wanted to know what our feces looked like and we resented it." Brother Joe, always the protector, suggested a compromise to the belligerent gathering. "It doesn't say 'our' specimen. It says only *a* specimen. So let's all choose up." They chose, Will Campbell remembered, "Eeny, meeny, miney, moe. Catch a nigger by the toe. If he hollers, make him pay, fifty dollars every day." Lots were drawn and the loser reluctantly provided the specimen. The state health authorities announced that *all* of the boys at East Fork were troubled by hookworm.

Mississippi and the South were changing, even if the protesters against the institutional tin boxes in Moore's pasture did not realize it. Will Campbell was on the last great dividing line between the old and new South. He was in the last of the Confederate generation, in the waning tales of Grandpa Bunt and the few remaining rebel veterans who sat on the courthouse square at Liberty, with their white beards, imposing gold watch chains, and canes. But he was also in the new generation which brought

WPA hot lunch programs to East Fork, the twenty-seat privy, and the new highway on old state route 24.

"That was the first money we ever had," Campbell mused. "The highway came through and paid my daddy five hundred dollars for the land involved in the right-of-way. We bought our first radio after daddy got paid, and every Saturday night we listened to the Grand Ole Opry."

The "new" dwelling with the bored well, up the road from the old place, housed myriad family memories of life and death, peace and turmoil.

Sometimes Will Campbell will reach for his guitar and half-sing, half-recite verses of the hard, early Mississippi years. There were tales of Grandma Bertha Parker,

> *Long auburn tresses dropping into the sourdough and teacake batter*
> *Like tongues of fire in reverse*
> *On Pentecost day.*
> *And dark roasted coffee beans,*
> *parched each morning*
> *And ground by the first hint of day in a cast iron grinder.*
> *Remember her saying:*
> *"Be kind to the Sissons.*
> *Skin don't make folks trash.*
> *They may be angels*
> *unaware.*
> *Some folks say I oughten to dip snuff."*
> *"I don't care if he's colored.*
> *And I don't care if he stole Earl Moore's old truck.*
> *He's fourteen years old,*
> *And they ain't gonna beat him."*

There were also songs about Uncle Coot:

> *Lying there with him at the end of the cotton row,*
> *Waiting for Aunt Ruth to bring water to her Boaz,*
> *Water in a bucket, still tasting like hog lard.*

"Don't believe I'll be a farmer when I grow up,
        Uncle Coot."
"What you gonna be, boy?"
"Believe I'll be a preacher."
"That's real good, boy.
That's real good.
But be a real one."

Be a real preacher. . . . When did it come? "Maybe when I was five years old and had pneumonia," Campbell recalled. Amite County had few doctors and precious few nurses to care for the frail child with the burning fever. "There was this woman named Miss Flora Calendar. In the community, she was known as the person who was good for tending the sick."

Lee Campbell paid the nurse twelve dollars a week, to come and stay, day and night. "Nobody thought I would make it," he said. "There were no drugs then—nothing but mustard plasters. So the nurse came into the house and ordered everybody out of the room—said they were breathing up too much oxygen. Mamma almost fired her then, and especially after Miss Flora threw open the windows in the dead of winter to let in a little air. But I lived."

He lived, to confess his sins two years later at the sweatbox East Fork Baptist church, and to be born again in the crystal waters of the Glory Hole. "You know," Campbell said, "when I lived after that sickness, that seemed to make a difference. Nobody expected me to live, since I was the puny one in the family. After that, everyone just figured that I had been given to the Lord. It was kind of a bargain. God let Will Davis live, so Will would be a preacher. It was almost as if my folks prayed that 'Lord he is the weak one in the litter and if You let him live, You can have him.' There wasn't much talk after that. Everybody just assumed from then on that I was going to be the Baptist preacher in the family."

The simple, framed certificate of ordination hangs on the kitchen wall of the old farmhouse. Will Davis Campbell was only seventeen, a recent graduate of the Little High School at East Fork. The local council of the Baptist Church was convened to test his faith. The gathering of churchmen included Campbell's father, uncle, cousin, and the local preacher.

They were convinced of his moral uprightness and signed his "orders." The certificate was typed on a small portable machine by the young preacher from the Louisiana Baptist school. Some of the words were misspelled—even the name "East Fork."

"Then I never gave a thought to moving far from home," Campbell says. "Nobody did that then, unless he took some job up in Memphis, or worked on a boat at New Orleans. I intended to be a Baptist preacher. You know, just the kind who lived in the community or somewhere around there. Raise a family. Hell, I planned to live and die there with my people, and just be a preacher."

The preaching had begun several months earlier in the small East Fork church. It was youth day for the graduating seniors of the high school, and for Will Campbell.

Everyone called him "Dave" in East Fork—sometimes "Little Dave." Nobody else would have been considered for the sermon. After all, he was the one called to preach. God, with Miss Flora Calendar's nursing help, had saved him from the fever. Evie Lee played hymns on the old piano. And the boy preacher rose to deliver his first sermon. He had practiced it for days in the corn patch at East Fork. Campbell had written it out in longhand and nailed it to the rung between two plow handles. Then he preached it to the horse. Campbell told the animal how the story of creation in the first chapter of Genesis compared to the new life facing the graduating seniors at East Fork.

Even then, Campbell was aware that he was different. "Here I was, a sixteen-year-old Baptist fundamentalist, expected to preach about salvation in some other life. But that first sermon was not the usual one, about how man from Adam was heaven-bound. Instead I preached about how the rest of the Bible, from the creation story to the end, talked about how people treated each other on earth." The sermon was called "In the Beginning."

It was the dawn of a realization, more latent than apparent, that Amite County was part of a South of paradoxes, good and evil, gentle and violent. Campbell was a Southern Baptist, expected to ignore the human condition and talk of the pleasures of heaven. But the reality was there in East Fork, where, when Campbell was a boy, the white-robed knights of the Ku Klux Klan solemnly entered the small church building and presented a pulpit Bible stamped "K.K.K."

When did it come first, that early awareness of being part of his Mississippi heritage, but not part at all? It rose out of story and song, not voiced by outsiders, but from within the very land itself.

There was, again, Grandpa Bunt Campbell who told tales of a Confederate army fighting to preserve a slave empire. But there was the day when John Walker, a black man walked down the road past Grandpa Bunt's house. Recently Walker had been beaten by some white men for stealing a sack of corn. When he trudged past the porch, Will Campbell and his friends yelled "Hey nigger, hey nigger." Grandpa Bunt, the teller of the Confederate tales, sat on a stump nearby. He motioned to the boys and stared at them. "Boys," he said, "there aren't any more niggers." "Yessir there are, grandpa," the Campbell brood protested. "One just walked down the road right now." The old man shook his head. "No, there aren't any more niggers. All the niggers are dead. All we have now are colored people."

It comes back in memory when Preacher Will Campbell strums the guitar in the hollow at Mt. Juliet. Tales of paradox, such as that of the country physician, Dr. Quinn. He would come with the black medical bag which smelled of chloroform and iodine, sometimes to examine the men in the community who had served in the First World War. After all, the government had decreed that any *disabled* veteran was worthy of a pension. To Dr. Quinn, they were all disabled:

Not kin
But friend

To everyone.
Had his shop in the East Fork Village.
Left behind a lot of bottles and things.
And standing on tip-toes peering and squinting
*   at them was exciting.*
Henry Ford moved him to Liberty—"Roll on civilization!"
(Some folks say there ain't no Liberty in Mississippi.)
But that's where we got our mail.
And that's where Dr. Quinn lived.
And there is Liberty in every county
*   where every veteran is disabled—even darkies.*

There were other sounds he remembered later more distinctly. Some came during the Sunday dinner at his Uncle Curt's farm, when a field hand burst through the kitchen door. A black tenant farmer, Noon Wells, a reputed womanizer, had been shot. Uncle Curt remained steadfast at the dinner table. After all, it was a black man who had died. Instead he ordered someone to say grace and the family finished the meal. Finally, he rose, and with Will Campbell and brother Joe tagging at his heels, drove to the tenant house two miles away. Campbell remembers the open bullet wound, the caked blood in the nostrils, and the flies crawling into the still, open mouth.

An hour later, the body remained on the front porch as Will Campbell heard voices. A long, weaving train of black women huddled by a pine stump as the crowd came into full view. Someone muttered "That's the dead boy's mother." The women came on, their voices rising and falling, first in whimpers and then loud groans of human agony. In the cabin clearing, the women who had supported Noon Wells' mother set her free, and she sat by the body of her son, brushing away the caked blood on his face and swatting furiously at the swarming insects.

Now Will Campbell recalls that vividly, but remembers more the incantations which the mourners had voiced on the dirt road. The mother would call, and her friends would answer:

LORD!
Lord
JEESUS!
Jesus
GOD LORD JESUS
Lord Jesus
TAKE ME ON TO GLORY.
On to glory.
OR BRING MY BABY HOME!
Bring 'im home.

Later Campbell remembered that "they were Jesus sounds. Just Jesus sounds—the pleas of one African peasant woman to the son of a Jewish peasant woman to be with her in the agony."

Even then, the earlier Jesus sounds of baptism at the Glory Hole were far removed. In a few years the young graduate of the East Fork school, the ordained Baptist preacher, went off to college. On the surface, the small Louisiana College at Pineville appeared to represent little change. It was still a hard-ankled Baptist fundamentalist school. Will Campbell remained a devout Baptist by the guidelines of an unwritten credo. He drove out on Sunday to preach the word at small Baptist churches. The preacher's pay was meager, but helped to defray his college expenses. Still, it was not enough. He met and married another student, tall slender Brenda Fisher, and the financial demands mounted. Long hours as a clerk in A. Ginsberg's drygoods store helped him earn a living.

But he was across the Mississippi River, the first step in a long changing from the tightly-knit attitudes of family and community in Amite County. Will Campbell was in the process of his long learning, that the South, with its patchwork culture of community, religion, and music is an absolute paradox which often races wildly between extremes. Like the spring winds which blow across the limestone rocks of Middle Tennessee, the forces which shaped the dichotomy are more elusive than are the results. No doubt some of the paradoxes were there before the Civil War which brought the tales of Grandpa Bunt Campbell.

As noted, there was the presence of slavery, of three-and-a-half million human chattels. They were a reminder that Dixie was caught up in the contrast between the older liberal heritage of Thomas Jefferson and his Declaration of Independence, and the newer preachments of John C. Calhoun, who spoke for the master class. A huge growth of Southern evangelical religion in the decades before the war underscored this extreme, so much so that people of the Baptist and Methodist faiths cut their ties with their Northern brethren.

Even the escapist literary romanticism of the decades before Bull Run may have accentuated the presence of stark opposites. The writings of Sir Walter Scott did provide an opiate, did indeed bolster a planter's self-image of grandeur, class and order. The perusal of *Rob Roy* and *Ivanhoe* by the uncertain light of a candle on a Mississippi plantation could serve as well to confirm the existence of a dichotomy in one's life. Outside the mansion house were opposites and others—several million slaves, huge numbers of rough-hewn egalitarian folk on the Dixie frontier, and millions of fellow whites, who, for reasons of faith or fortune, did not belong to the master class. The planter's own existence also involved contradictions. Proud displays of the chivalric code could not erase the reality that some of the slaveocracy were nouveaux riches from less than elegant backgrounds, or that the big house was often not a palatial manor but a large frame dwelling in a cleared thicket, imperiled by the same typhoid fever, mosquitoes, milk sickness, and loneliness which shadowed more humble abodes.

The experience of total defeat in the Civil War did much to accentuate the Southern paradox, more perhaps than any other factor. After the war, the South turned with zeal to the burgeoning evangelical faiths—Southern Baptist, Methodist, Presbyterian, Pentecostals, and the rising strength of the Disciples of Christ. By 1900, three of every four Southerners espoused faiths which enforced a Janus-like self-image. Man was good and bad;

existence was travail on earth and rapture in Heaven; Jesus provided comfort in the Lamb's bosom, but God's wrath at sinners
conjured up feelings of guilt and insecurity.

No wonder that the white Southern mind often became a yok-
ing together of opposites which often were extremes. It is still
the bedrock of the Bible Belt but possesses a statistically vali-
dated heritage of violence. Traditional Dixie individualism is
countered by a tradition of repressing freethinkers—abolitionists
and other reformers, evolutionists, political liberals, and human
rights advocates. The land boasts one of the greatest literary traditions in America, the epoch of the Southern Renascence of the
1930s, a rich harvest of writers such as William Faulkner, Thomas
Wolfe, Robert Penn Warren, and a score of others. Yet the same
state of Mississippi which spawned Faulkner, Eudora Welty, and
Will Campbell consistently leads the nation in rates of illiteracy
and low expenditures for education.

Everywhere one is confronted with contradictions. A rever-
ence for the soil is mixed with a heritage of poor conservation,
strip mining, and the deliberate burning of forests. The lingering
roots of the agrarian ethos is countered by a chamber of commerce boosterism, hawking the wares of every crossroads hamlet
to some industrial concern. The much caricatured slow pace of
life is interrupted by the frenetic roar of that Southerner's passion, the automobile. Deep religious piety and repressive sexual
attitudes are matched with raw carnality. The reputation for ease
and hospitality is juxtaposed with a suspicion of outsiders and
the dark currents of a capacity for violence. The ultimate place
of paradox in the South, as we have seen, is the religious-music
empire at Nashville. The city is as much a mood as it is a place.
It is a feeling which arises from the interwoven fabric of many
things—the lingering reminders of the Confederate heritage, vis-
ible remnants of a genteel Old South, deep moods of guilt and
repression arising from the pulpits of fundamentalist churches,
the bustle of New South commercial fervor, an earthy river-town
sensuality, the melodic heritage of the music of William the gardener, a strong passion for the land, and firm roots in a rural,

religious background which extend across the countryside to countless small, white-framed churches. Culturally, Will Campbell's Nashville is a city of conflicting images which often collide. It is a place which has never made peace with a multifaced environment.

Will Campbell was on the road to Nashville, even years before he left the tiny community of East Fork. Today, on the farm at Mt. Juliet, he is more troubador than preacher, a balladeer of the human condition as viewed through Southern eyes. Often his lectures at universities are interspersed with melodies from Music Row. "These people are the poets," he remarked. "Country music is people music—honest, liberal, and the only true American art form. It is also theologically sound, meaning Orthodox. You see, in a typical performance the country singer accepts the doctrine of original sin—that the world is all fouled up. But if you listen to the closing number, which they always call the "song of inspiration," they always end up by admitting that the real hope of changing anything is beyond the control of some local church's steering committee."

The winds of agony and turmoil which eventually brought both the music and Will Campbell to Nashville blew across the Cumberland River country even before the Civil War when Nashville was a brawling Ohio Valley river town, with a waterfront of saloons and bordellos. Then, in 1862, the river brought the Yankee gunboats and the finery of Old South Nashville began to show wear. The spacious mansions were seized as Yankee army headquarters or hospitals and fashionable lawns were denuded of trees for breastworks or firewood. The population was also changing, because, for almost all of the Civil War, Nashville was an occupied city. Northern soldiers and business entrepreneurs came, and some stayed after Appomattox to help guide the rising New South battle for banking, insurance, and river commerce. Thousands of other newcomers arrived also—prostitutes, gamblers, and misfits who fed upon the army of occupation. By 1863, the reported rate of venereal disease among federal soldiers averaged twenty-eight cases a day, and once a boatload of 150 prostitutes was sent downriver to Kentucky, only to be returned by the citizens of Louisville.

The raw hedonism of a river-town culture was interrupted in the decades after the war by the arrival of another element. Thousands of rural people migrated to Nashville from the farm valleys of the Duck, Elk, Stones, and Caney Fork rivers. With them came the rising tide of evangelical fervor that was surging all across Dixie, and the population of Southern Baptists and other fundamentalist faiths grew in rapidly accelerating numbers in Nashville. Their outcries against drinking, dancing, fornication and other assorted transgressions were shouted from pulpits and embellished by tabernacle evangelists such as Sam Jones. Jones even reached out to the river-town element, and converted a steamboat captain named Tom Ryman. Ryman promptly erected a huge revival hall on modern-day Fifth Avenue, not far from the river landing. In 1940, the barn-like brick structure, the Ryman Auditorium, became the home of the Grand Ole Opry.

Even by the late nineteenth century, there were street sounds in Nashville, voices later to be Will Campbell's people and the roots of country music. On some corners, itinerant ballad singers who had migrated from rural hamlets sang the native American ballads which told stories of murder, labor violence, and railroad tragedies. Many wrote their own material and sold it to listeners on small cards called "pallets." Early performers also learned their trade from the vaudeville-type singers on Nashville's streets.

Nearby church and tabernacle auditoriums thundered with another touchstone of country music. There were camp meetings and revival songs such as "Amazing Grace" which erupted from the Great Revival on the frontier fifty years before the Civil War. Some were white spirituals out of the Southern uplands, melodies which bespoke a fatalistic resolution coming from a hard land where the soil did not yield easily to the plow or to the gravedigger's spade. Sometimes the rudiments of musical knowledge displayed by these singers came from rural musical conventions and schools held in backwater villages by itinerant singing masters. From the late nineteenth century until after the First World War, the South was alive with small medicine shows, black-face minstrel troups, and variety offerings which reached into remote areas, to schoolhouse grounds and county square barbecues.

All of this was part of Will Campbell's musical heritage as a boy in East Fork. When his father obtained the money to purchase a radio, the family listened faithfully to WSM Radio and the Grand Ole Opry. In part, Campbell heard the amalgam of the music of Southern whites—traditional Appalachian folk music, religious camp meeting tunes, and vaudeville entertainers.

Will Campbell heard another kind of music on Nashville's streets—Jesus sounds, which were not unlike the voices Campbell and his brother Joe had heard on the day the black tenant farmer was murdered in the Mississippi cottonland. The black heritage of the Delta blues reaches back to the high-pitched, solo voices of slave work-gangs in the Mississippi Delta. After the Civil War, some black freedmen moved northward with their music. Rooted in slavery, religion, and an earthy, humane quality, the original sounds of the blues swept across the upper Southland and became an integral part of Will Campbell's Southern music.

Today Campbell maintains, "I am just a preacher." His flock is large and varied, but the bedrock of the flock has remained composed of two groups: downtrodden Southern white and black people.

Symbolically, the union of Will Campbell's parishioners came during a hot July week in 1927 in the small East Tennessee mountain community of Bristol. Nashville was years away from enjoying a reputation as the center of country music, and most recording was done by field teams armed with primitive equipment. Within a week, a Victor records talent scout in Bristol captured the melodies of the two country-music acts destined to become the most famous in America during the next decade—a mountain trio from Virginia called the Carter Family and a Mississippi solo artist, Jimmie Rodgers.

The Carter Family came to Bristol with a tradition of white rural music garnered from the tough mountainous slopes of Scott County, Virginia. Their songs—a blend of British and native American ballads, religious melodies, and Vaudeville tunes—contained the common elements of nostalgia and unfulfillment. Jimmie Rodgers also had these ingredients, but he added the flavor of his experience to the music of black laborers in Mississippi.

The differences in the two musical types heard by Will Campbell on his family's radio involved more than stylistic variations. True, the Delta Blues was a solo effort delivered in a high, wavering "blues shout," while the Appalachian strains of the Carter Family was harmony. A black blues singer relied upon a guitar played in "sock chord fashion," while the mountain whites played a medley of instruments. Also, the blues minstrel did not deliver the traditional four-line stanza of the white, British–American ballad; the Mississippi laborer sang in three-line stanzas, the first two lines presenting a problem, the final line the resolution.

More important, the blues of Will Campbell's Mississippi was music of the first person. Absent were the generalized themes of nostalgia and tragedy which had befallen some faceless person. The black singers talked of human problems in a more direct and personal manner, if not in a more honest fashion. Often the songs were laments of one's unhappy love relationships, poverty, or encounters with the law, all delivered in an earthy, sensual manner. This was the forerunner of the personal "lyric lament," which emerged strongly in the music of country-singer Hank Williams, and became the mainstream of Nashville music.

A direct line can be drawn from the early blues singers to Jimmie Rodgers, and eventually to the honky-tonk variety of country music heard by Will Campbell in the Second World War years. The last black street-troubadour was still on Nashville's streets when Campbell arrived in the late 1950s. For some twenty-five years, Cortelia Clark sat along Fifth Avenue with a battered guitar. His sightless eyes stared out into nowhere as he sang the three-line blues stanzas in a raspy voice. Most of the shoppers and businessmen in Fifth Avenue's bustle ignored him. For years the music industry overlooked Cortelia Clark and the entire black heritage in country songs. For a brief time in the 1960s, the blind street minstrel gained national attention when an enterprising music producer recorded his songs. But that did not last very long, and Cortelia Clark was again a street beggar on Fifth Avenue.

A movement began with those Bristol recording sessions in 1927. And Nashville could no longer ignore the strong winds of change which came with the years of the Second World War. Will Campbell's people would be heard. A nasal-voiced singer named Roy Acuff gained national attention with his melodies of nostalgia, religion, and unfulfilled love in the tradition of poor Southern Appalachian white people. Another Nashville performer, Ernest Tubb, personified the Jimmie Rodgers tradition in a blend of white country and black blues. Frank, direct lyrics addressed life's real problems for the rural Southerners and factory workers—alcoholism, poverty, and adultery. Eventually both musical types would emerge in the strains of a modern country music which would bring writers, publishers, recording technicians, and others by the thousands to Nashville between 1950 and 1960.

But the real catalyst was the Second World War, which took Will Campbell to the South Pacific and brought him face-to-face with the contradictions of his Amite Country heritage. Meanwhile, Campbell's people, black and white, were on the move. They became part of the vast cultural upheaval in the South which was brought about by the war and the social revolution of the 1940s.

Pearl Harbor loosened the bonds of a traditional Dixie life pattern centered on a nontransient world of family and community. Millions of Southerners now joined other Americans in great migrations: to California army camps and far-flung military outposts in the South Pacific; to shipyards in Mobile, Alabama, or

San Diego; to the petrochemical empire on the Gulf coast, steel mills in Pennsylvania and tank factories in Michigan. Southern ghettoes were spawned in Cleveland, Detroit, and Cincinnati, while thousands of rural and blue-collar workers left their farms and moved into Nashville, Birmingham, and other cities of the old South. And they demanded Will Campbell's music.

The war produced a revolution in country music which was carried to the California army camps, Texas roadhouses, and the neighborhood taverns in Southern enclaves in the North and the East. It was a revolution brought about by millions of noninheritors who demanded a simple, direct music which would express the tensions filling their lives in this time of immense social change. It was, as some writers have suggested, a "people music," which voiced openly the people's bewilderment with the social Armageddon of the 1940s: the changing sexual mores, rising divorce rates, alcoholism, infidelity, lonely separations from wives and children, or families uprooted from their heritage.

Such problems were never couched in vague lyrics, because the troubles were very real ones. They were the strains felt by an Ohio factory worker missing his family who had remained behind on a poor West Virginia farm; the gnawing questions of marital fidelity which faced both an Alabama soldier in a California camp and his wife who now labored in a Birmingham steel plant; and the long hours of drinking and feeding coins into a jukebox by an Appalachian migrant in a Detroit tavern.

Sometimes Will Campbell sits in the barber chair in the log office across the small creek from the old house and fingers the guitar. "Those people sing about the truth," he said. "They talk about motel rooms and cheating, or about the worker on the auto assembly line who sneaks vodka into his coffee. Hell, I never paid much attention to country music in those days. I mean right after the war, that was my period of pseudosophistication. I wore a tweed cap and smoked a big pipe. I acted the way a good liberal was supposed to act at Yale Divinity School. I didn't really understand it until I moved to Nashville in the 1950s and realized finally that it was people music—that these people tell about life as it is."

Country music and its cultural baggage were exasperating for the safe middle-class Nashville world of the 1940s. There was applause, in 1943, when the governor of Tennessee refused to speak at the inaugural of extended network radio broadcasts of the Grand Ole Opry, explaining that such music was turning Nashville into the world's hillbilly capital. There was horror when Roy Acuff entered the gubernatorial race in 1948, and criticism when another governor publicly sang the "Tennessee Waltz." The local gentry chuckled at the typical singer's attire of the gaudy leather-tooled boots, outrageous cowboy hats, and coats studded with rhinestones. Musicians were presumed to be illiterates who never paid their bills, went on drunken sprees while on road trips, and wore silly outfits. Musicians lived in shabby trailer parks north of the Cumberland River on Dickerson Road, or took meals at aging boarding houses in East Nashville. Their social life was not the Belle Meade Country Club but Tootsie's Orchid Lounge on Broad Street. Five days a week, the music people were out of sight and mind. Then they toured in huge DeSotos and elongated station wagons, with fiddles and guitars strapped on top. They were performing at small, rural motion-picture theaters reeking of stale popcorn, at county fairs, and at fish fries. Then on Saturday they came home to embarrass middle-class Nashville again, by reminding a national audience on the Grande Ole Opry that the city was indeed the world's hillbilly capital.

Or perhaps the contradictions in the music came too close to home. It is a music of paradoxes, and even the rural and blue-collar workers of the 1940s, who were its first audience, reflected this. They were the supporters of family, flag, and country, violently opposed to untraditional verities. Yet the themes of the music they loved expressed the opposites of their avowed values. The melodies delivered onstage at the Grand Ole Opry were filled with contradictions—loyal, docile wives and temptresses,

Southern Baptist faith and alcoholism, nostalgic tales of family life and broken marriages.

It was a religious service. Campbell talked for awhile, and then produced a guitar and sang. One song was "Catfish John," which told of the young white boy in Mississippi who had not understood why his elders disliked the lad's accompanying the fisherman to the riverbank. Catfish John was a former black slave from Vicksburg, traded once for a chestnut mare. He followed with "Hello Darling." Then there came "Red Necks, White Sox and Blue Ribbon Beer," a ballad of lonely Southern people in a roadside tavern, half-defiant, half-fearful of their rejection by middle-class society.

The Nashville middle class rejected, as well, the brilliant, erratic Hank Williams who had come to Nashville in 1949. He had been brought up on a poor Alabama farm much like that of the Campbells' at East Fork. Some of his songs came from the Baptist sweatbox church, others from the radio beamed toward Nashville. But Williams had also listened to the Jesus sounds of the mother of Noon Wells and her mourner companions, brought to him in the blues lament of the Montgomery black street singer called Teetot.

By 1950, Williams had become the first superstar of Nashville's music. More than that, he had become the bridge between the genres of country and popular music. Eight of his compositions, such as "Your Cheating Heart" and "Jambalaya," were recorded by popular artists, and suddenly the entire American music world began to notice Nashville. It was the start of a cultural revolution which, beginning in the mid-1950s, would bring thousands of music industry personnel to Nashville. But Williams was unable to cope with the differences between his tenant farm background and the glitter of Nashville, between the Baptist heritage and his guilt-ridden awareness of the society of the music world, and his star crashed. In 1952, the owners of the Grand Ole Opry fired him; within six months he was dead.

Perhaps it was not merely Hank Williams's behavior which

threatened the religious-business complex. Maybe they saw him only as an aberration of their own paradoxes, of what they had been in the rural South and on Little Wall Street in Nashville. Or perhaps the threat became a reality, when he moved among them into a garish home with gold-plated bathroom fixtures, out on fashionable Franklin Pike.

Hank Williams was only a small part of the vast onrushing tide of people who were surging to and from the Southland . . . from dusty army camps . . . in and out of a black ghetto in Detroit and a poor white Appalachian confine in Cleveland. They were all Will Campbell's people, although he was yet to know this. In 1943, when Campbell left Bible-bound Louisiana College and volunteered for military service, his own winds of change were sweeping across the Mississippi delta, winds which would eventually lead him also to Nashville.

MIDDAY

Years later, Will Campbell would admit that he never knew when the alienation began. "I never realized any real divide between my family and me when I first started preaching in Amite County. I had never intended to do anything but be a part of that culture. And when I left Louisiana College to join the army, I felt the same way.

I don't really know what changed me. It is easy to say that it came during the war when I read Howard Fast's *Freedom Road*. That was an important part of my life, but it would be an exaggeration to say that reading that one book turned my whole life around. And I would say my experiences with black soldiers had a lot to do with it, too, even though our units remained segregated until after 1945. Sure the war had a lot to do with my ideas. I remember when I first returned home for visits, older folks would listen to my ideas and actually be pretty sympathetic. 'Oh,' they would say, 'he's saying that just because he's a veteran and is a little crazy right now. Just let him get home for awhile and he'll forget all those ideas.' "

Instead, Campbell left home for college, and later went to Yale to study ethics under Liston Pope. "I know I was in my era of pseudosophistication, when you would never admit you enjoyed country music, for example. Even then I was not aware of the gulf between my upbringing and where I was. I still intended to live in the Mississippi area for the rest of my life."

Campbell felt no conscious discontent with his heritage. "I never rejected Mississippi, even in the days when I sported a tweed cap and a big curved pipe. My roots were too deep. Instead, what happened was a conflict which I had to deal with when I returned to my first—and only—church in Taylor, Louisiana." After all, the family in Amite County had urged him to go off and get *the* best education. "It turned out to be a conflict I still have to deal with," he said. "I did what everybody wanted me to do—went off to Tulane, Yale, and elsewhere. But that very thing—the education—cut me off from doing what I originally set out to do: to just be a Baptist preacher at some church in the Deep South."

Later Campbell would insist that no Southerner growing up in such a tightly knit environment of family, religion, and community can ever leave it. "You can't deny such a thing: to deny you have left home completely is nothing more than to affirm that you have not." As an example, he recalled his days at Wake Forest College, when his wife Brenda joined him nightly for dinner in the college dining hall. "Brenda always wanted to sit back in some dark corner," Campbell said. "Well, at the time I thought she wanted to do something a little romantic—just the two of us alone. Finally I realized the *real* reason was because I always crumbled my biscuit in a glass of milk—just like we did always back home in Mississippi. There I was, the big college man, quoting philosophy while we ate, and crumbling my biscuit just like I did on Grandpa Bunt's farm."

Still, he was moving on a collision course between the Southerner's past and present, the essence of that inbred feeling of alienation. He was at Yale in 1952, when the United States Supreme Court began deliberations on *Brown* v. *Board of Education.* "We divinity students from the Deep South figured we had all the answers. And I remember we were disappointed when we learned the court had taken on the case then, and expected the whole issue would be decided before we could get home to participate."

So he came home to Taylor, Louisiana, but it was not home at all. Two things were different now. "Even then, in that first and only church, I didn't preach the kind of sermon they wanted." In 1954, the year the United States Supreme Court upheld the *Brown* v. *Board of Education* decision on integration, Will Davis Campbell resigned. He moved to the University of Mississippi as the Southern Baptist chaplain on campus.

"When I went to Ole Miss as chaplain, I did not consider myself to be a civil rights activist. In fact, I have never considered myself a leader in the civil rights movement, even though the family back in Amite County thought so. Frankly, I was never interested in what people call 'race relations.' To me it was not a matter of race at all: it was a matter of Christian principles."

Nor did Campbell journey to Ole Miss to begin a conscious break with his past. "I went there because I wanted to live in Mississippi," he remembered. "I had a job offer as chaplain at the University of Oklahoma at the same time, and some of my divinity school friends thought I was crazy for not taking it."

Campbell arrived at the university in August 1954, three months after the Brown decision was handed down by the Supreme Court. In those first months across the South, there was a general shock of disbelief, mingled with the assertions of Dixie political leaders that the decision was ridiculous. Senator James Eastland of Mississippi insisted that the Court had been brainwashed by "left-wing pressure groups." In Georgia, segregationist candidate Marvin Griffin won election to the state house by denouncing "meddlers, demagogues, race baiters, and Communists" who had determined to search out and destroy Dixie's principles of state's rights. In Texas, Allan Shivers won the governorship on a platform which included strong denouncements of the NAACP. "Still, in those first months, nobody took the thing seriously," Campbell said. "Many whites in Mississippi thought desegregation was a joke. There was a standard tale going around of the local principal who was asked by town officials, 'How many niggers are you going to have in your school next term?' 'About twice what I had last year,' the principal laughed. 'And twice nothing is nothing.' ''

Then came the dark year of 1955. Sometimes Campbell still strums the guitar and sings a melody he wrote about his world that was going mad in 1955. The song tells of a young man who rode the rails from Mississippi to Chicago because the madness of white and black people in Mississippi was getting him down. The final chorus was a prayer:

> *Then that Mississippi madness, be Mississippi magic again.*
> *That Mississippi madness, be Mississippi magic again.*
> *'Fore we was born we was all kin.*
> *When we dead we'll be kinfolks again.*

In reality, Uncle Tom was dead, and scores of local petitions were being filed by NAACP groups demanding that the Supreme Court decision be implemented. A massive bus boycott erupted in Montgomery, Alabama. From Arkansas to South Carolina, local black groups astonished their old masters by threats of economic pressure. It was the beginning of a period of social upheaval, and Will Campbell's people fought back in fear and anger.

By 1955, the White Citizens' Council was taking control of Mississippi. Power came to it slowly at first. The first council in Mississippi—and anywhere in the South—was organized on a hot July day in 1954 in the delta town of Indianola. "A local circuit judge named Tom Brady was scheduled to make a speech to the Sons of the American Revolution in Greenwood. En route, he stopped by the Ole Miss campus and asked to speak with Dean Malcolm Guess, who was my predecessor as Baptist chaplain. Dean Guess was retired, but had an office on campus. Brady asked him to read the speech. He did, and then Brady went on to deliver his address."

Campbell met Dean Guess only minutes after the meeting with

Tom Brady. "He looked somber and I asked him why. Dean Guess said, " 'You'll know soon enough, because that's a speech that will be heard for a long, long time.' "

The speech was turned into a pamphlet entitled *Black Monday*, which became the handbook of the entire White Citizens' Council movement throughout Mississippi and elsewhere. The theme was simplistic: White people were a superior race endowed with the right to rule an inferior people. It was a reassertion of the old pre-Civil War Stoic philosophy of the benevolent master and the docile slave. "The Southern negro knows we are his friend," *Black Monday* insisted. But the Supreme Court's decision "will start a conflagration in the South which all of Neptune's mighty ocean cannot quench."

As to be expected, the July meeting in Indianola was not a gathering of poor, uneducated white men. They were bankers, attorneys, and cotton magnates. The movement had begun. By October 1954, twenty Mississippi counties were organized along the credo of *Black Monday*, and a state organization was formed. The summer of 1955 produced 60,000 council members. Within the next three years, the council controlled state politics. Finally in 1960, a long-time council member, Ross R. Barnett, was elected governor.

By 1956, Will Campbell had resigned his position at the University of Mississippi. "It was not one thing," he said, "only a series of incidents which made me realize that I could not live there anymore."

Initially, he became involved with a communal group called Providence Farm. The farm had been organized in the 1930s by young churchmen who had come under the influence of Reinhold Niebuhr. Primarily it served as a clinic for poor black people in a desolate area of Holmes County. "It had been there a long time, but given the excitement of the times in the fifties, everything got blown out of proportion. Word got around that they didn't have separate doors and waiting rooms for whites and blacks. Then a story started that they had integrated swimming. The truth was that the kids swam in this dangerous creek and they had bought a bathing suit for a black maid so she would watch them. Pretty soon the local authorities and the Citizens' Council types were putting a lot of pressure on those people, and I decided to drive down and see what was going on.

"I found that the farm was under siege," Campbell remembered. Farm leaders told him that a posse of local citizens had come to warn them to leave the county. Meanwhile, telephone lines were cut repeatedly. A roadblock prevented blacks from reaching the clinic, and, at the point where the farm driveway intersected with the county road, another posse kept anyone from entering or leaving the clinic. Campbell crossed the blockade, but was stopped at night when he left Providence Farm. "They didn't say anything to me, just shined a flashlight in my eyes, then walked around and took down my license number. Then they let me go." By the next morning, an irate state senator was on campus, demanding to know *what* one of the university's staff was doing at Providence Farm. Campbell was called into the administrative office and questioned by a friendly dean. "I remember he said, 'Will, we don't want you to think we're scared or are being critical of you, but we have got to give those folks an answer as to what you were doing there.' "

It was Campbell's first contact with the bonds of fear tightening around Mississippi, and it made him realize how far removed he was from his heritage. "I told the dean what the farm was, and said that I was frightened that fascism had reached our own country, where a Christian couldn't even drive across a county line to visit some fellow brethren without being intimidated."

The intimidation had only begun. In 1956, a university committee, which included Campbell, made plans for the annual Religious Emphasis Week. "I was determined to invite some speakers who were sympathetic to racial justice." An invitation went out to Alvin Kershaw, an Episcopal priest from Ohio. "Everybody was pleased with Kershaw's coming," Campbell remembered. "He was a television celebrity then—had appeared on the television program *The Sixty-Four Thousand Dollar Question* and had won a lot of money."

The problem arose when Kershaw announced publicly that he intended to give part of his earnings to the NAACP. Mississippi newspapers roared with anger in front-page stories of how the university was inviting a donor to the NAACP. One night, while visiting a colleague, Campbell was interrupted by a university policeman who escorted him to the chancellor's home. Campbell was told in polite but firm language that Kershaw's appearance had to be cancelled. Instead, the speakers would consist of local ministers at Oxford. However, the ministers rallied around Campbell: not one agreed to come. "Instead, I issued a public statement, that every day at the appointed hour for the speakers, I would go to the university chapel and meditate on the things which had brought us to such a sad day at Ole Miss." He went every day, and each morning, several hundred people—college faculty members, students, and townspeople—quietly filed in to sit with Campbell.

That was the beginning of years of harassment, late-night obscene telephone calls, hate mail, and veiled threats on his life. A local black minister came to Campbell's office in the university YMCA building one evening for a visit. While he was there, the two men walked by a Ping-Pong table and decided to play a game. Then Campbell noticed a staff member watching from the doorway with a friend. "I recognized the guy. He was a big fellow who had played football and had a reputation for being a rabid segregationist, and now worked on the staff in the personnel department." Nothing was said then. Campbell drove the minister back to his church. "I took back streets and circled the town twice. I was afraid someone would follow and try to make trouble for my friend." When he returned to the Ole Miss campus, the two men confronted Campbell by some shrubbery outside the YMCA building. "Hell, I was scared," Campbell said. "The big guy pushed forward toward me and said 'Okay, was he a nigger?' I replied that if they couldn't tell the difference, what difference could it make? He kept shouting 'Goddamit, was he a nigger' and I kept walking faster toward the administration building. I really thought he was going to beat me up.

"I knew my boss, the dean of student personnel, would call me in, so that night I went to see him first. He told me I had used bad judgment in playing Ping-Pong with my friend on the campus." The next morning, the front lawn of Campbell's house was littered with Ping-Pong balls, painted half-white, half-black.

"Maybe the punch bowl incident was the last straw," Campbell said. "Our staff was having a party for new students in the YMCA building. It was a week before the Ping-Pong incident." One of the campus chaplains called Campbell aside and pointed to the punch bowl. Someone had placed a cup of human feces, sprinkled with powdered sugar, in the bowl. Campbell complained to the assistant chancellor who insisted there was no way to discover who had fouled the punch bowl. "Funny," Campbell recalled. "The fellow used to work for the Justice Department, was once first assistant to J. Edgar Hoover. He could catch most wanted criminals but couldn't discover who dumped crap in a punch bowl."

It was time to leave Mississippi.

"I told my brother Joe first." He was a druggist in Meridian, and drove up to meet Will in a small all-night cafe in Eupora, Mississippi. As small boys, Joe had always been the strong one, the protector of the frail, younger Will, and he still assumed that role. When Campbell told him about the goings-on at Ole Miss, Joe exploded. "Goddamit, Will, you are going to get yourself killed up there!" "I remember I told Joe that they didn't kill white folks in Mississippi—just blacks. He looked at me and said 'Before this whole thing is over with, they will. You'll see.' "

"The irony is," Campbell said, "he was worried about me, and I was beginning to worry about Joe. He worked long, hard hours as a druggist in Meridian, and had begun to take some of his own pills, uppers and downers, just to keep going." Later, the tragedy of his brother's death would play a major role in Campbell's disillusionment with society's formal institutions of state, church, and reform organizations.

But that was several years in the future, after Campbell had stepped into the mainstream of the civil rights controversy. The decision was made that night in the little cafe: Will Campbell was leaving Mississippi. The National Council of Churches had decided to establish a Southern Office of the Department of Racial and Cultural Relations, and Campbell had been offered a position. "I would be a troubleshooter, more or less," Campbell recalled. "I would visit trouble spots, see people in jail, practically do anything I wanted to do. They even gave me the option of setting up the office anywhere I wanted to."

His brother Joe pleaded vainly for Campbell to refuse the position. "Brother, don't take that job. Man, you'll get killed for sure. That's like saying you're going to work for the Communist Party or something down here. You're just jumping from the frying pan into the fire!"

Not long afterwards, Will Campbell left Mississippi with his wife Brenda and their children. "I had never planned to leave home," Campbell said later. "Now I know there is no way I would ever return."

Will Campbell came to Nashville in 1956 and established his new office in the old Belmont section along Music Row. Even now he cannot say why he left Mississippi while others stayed. "I can talk about the army experience and the reading of *Freedom Road*, like I said, but I really don't know. Maybe it goes back way beyond that, to that time when Grandpa Bunt told us 'There are no more niggers—just colored people.' But why me? I wasn't alone that day, when he sat on the stump and lectured us; must have been fifteen of us around. Why did it hit me and not the others?"

His family must have wondered the same thing. A few kinsmen did not have Grandpa Bunt's tolerance. Some were even local Klansmen. White robes or not, the family recoiled in shock when Campbell became a civil rights activist.

For seven years Campbell was involved in the struggle for black rights. His job was that of a troubleshooter, moving in and out of areas seething with racial strife. Before long, Campbell found himself in the forefront. In 1956, he was in the East Tennessee mountain community of Anderson when court-ordered integration in the public schools caused a riot. The same year the courts demanded that a young black woman, Autherine Lucy, be admitted to the University of Alabama. Militant, well-organized segregationists fanned the campus and town of Tuscaloosa into a frenzy. Mobs dominated the campus, while the state police did little, except to remove "Miss Lucy" from the the university.

Back in East Fork, Mississippi, family members grumbled as newspapers reported his activities. "What's happened to Dave Campbell?" some asked. Others began sending letters or making telephone calls expressing their shock.

They were shocked even more when Campbell became a comrade to hated black activists, such as Martin Luther King, Jr., Ralph Abernathy, Fred Shuttlesworth, Andrew Young, Bayard Rustin, and a score of others. He was already a friend of Martin Luther King, Jr., when, in 1956, a group of prominent black leaders convened in Atlanta to organize the Southern Christian Leadership Conference. King had been forced to leave the conference early because of threats against his family, and was not there when Will Campbell arrived. Even to black activists, Preacher Will Campbell appeared a strange figure, clad in a modest suit and the black preacher's hat, and bearing, always, the necessary walking stick, guitar case, Bible, and bottle of bourbon. When Campbell arrived at the meeting, he was the only white man present and some overenthusiastic young black organizers refused him admittance. Then Bayard Rustin walked into the hall and spotted Campbell. "Let this man in," he demanded. "We need *him*."

During his remaining years of work for the National Council of Churches, Will Campbell walked with Southern Stoicism through masses of angry, heaving humanity in the long civil rights turmoil. He went to Little Rock, Arkansas, in 1957, when Governor Orval E. Faubus had surrounded Central High School with armed National Guardsmen. Campbell and a handful of others escorted the young black students through the jeering mob to the school's entrance, where they were denied admission.

No one in Campbell's household ever knew where he would turn up next. Sometimes he would leave to negotiate with businessmen in Birmingham and go on to Atlanta for more meetings of the Southern Christian Leadership Conference; then, back to Birmingham, to console the black families who had lost children when a Baptist church was bombed. In Montgomery, Campbell ministered to the wounded Freedom Riders in 1961. He was at the University of Mississippi after the fearful riot, in 1962, caused by the admission of the black student, James Meredith. Campbell was present during demonstrations in Birmingham and Albany, and during the long march from Selma to Montgomery. Or he would be on speaking tours in Northern cities, where he encouraged others to enlist in the crusade taking place in Dixie.

Meanwhile, some family members in Amite County disowned him. He did not return to Mississippi often, and close relatives and friends urged him to stay away. They did not understand him, and he in turn had grown apart from them. In these few years, the myriad images culled from the stubborn earth at East Fork—of Grandpa Bunt, the government-financed outdoor toilets, the salvation yells at the Glory Hole—became remote for him. "I had lost my roots for a time," Campbell mused later. "Hell, I could cuss rednecks, crackers, and Southern sheriffs with the best of them."

By the early 1960s, Will Campbell's message was in the process of radical change. He had come to believe that the *real* foe of the downtrodden black was not the White Citizens' Council or the Klan. Instead, he was slowly becoming committed to an absolute return to a primitive form of the Christian faith, one void of institutional strictures. "Institutions have always divided mankind," Campbell said. What do institutions create? In a speech to a Virginia religious gathering, Campbell spelled it out. "The ashes of 200,000 people lie quiet in Hiroshima. An old black man sits in Arkansas, worrying about the safety of his daughter in a viciously racist society. A middle-aged white man is afraid and frustrated in North Carolina and turns to hating and joins the KKK because the world neither needs nor likes rednecks anymore. Two men sit in a jail in the mountains to prove their commitment in the Lord by handling copperheads and rattlesnakes. A brokenhearted mother grieves alone in Orange County, California, because her son has been murdered by the state. . . ."

Everywhere Campbell turned, he saw the evils of institutional control. In an essay called "Which Way for Southern Churches: Footwashing or the New Hermeneutic," Campbell lashed out at the failure of formal religion in the South to cope with the racial crisis. "If we are to be honest," he complained, "we must admit that at the congregational level, the white church in the South has not yet had the slightest involvement in the racial crisis." Why was it, he asked, that only "a few pastors have joined an occasional march," but little else was accomplished.

Campbell's answer was that the Southern Baptist faith and other powerful regional churches had become too involved in their institutional structure. No one wanted to return to the street techniques of First Century Christianity. "We rejected fundamentalism and turned away from seeking answers in the Scriptures. We have retreated into the sophistication of the new hermeneutics"—a reference to the German biblical scholarship that seemed to be making the Scriptures a preserve of professional academicians.

It was an early foray into the struggle he would lead in later years, in an attempt to strip religion bare of formalism and return to the primitivism of basic principles of Christian humanity. Later, in an essay entitled "Can There Be a Crusade for Christ," Campbell and James Holloway attacked mass evangelical religious rallies. To Campbell, large-scale religious crusades, such as those of Billy Graham, were not based upon the principles of the simplicity of Jesus' teachings. "Politics and culture are the 'Christ' for all crusades. . . . There can be no 'decisions' for Christ in

crusades. There can only be *enlistments* by individuals, institutions, structures, and movements into ideological causes, into the
political maneuverings which are a fundamental part of the suffering, slavery, and death in our, and every, civilization."

By the early 1960s, Campbell's experience on university campuses had led him to believe that educational institutions were
guilty of the same strictures as the churches. "There is no such
thing as academic freedom on a campus," he said. "Go to a major
Southern university such as Emory or Vanderbilt and I bet you
every professor in the divinity school has his degree from one of
five universities." Institutions exist to perpetuate themselves. That
was what Campbell was coming to believe. "Do you think the
people at a school like Vanderbilt would allow someone on their
faculty from some fundamentalist school like Bob Jones University? Maybe Bob Jones wouldn't take a Vanderbilt graduate
either, but, then again, the folks at those ultraconservative schools
aren't the ones who beat their breasts about academic freedom."

Besides, Campbell asserts, the large institutions are the ones
who trained the generals, technocrats, and others who put
America in Vietnam. "Who do you think trained the generals
who killed thousands in the rice paddies or educated the people
who invented chemical warfare? They didn't come from those
pitiful little schools everyone labels as redneck. They came from
the Harvards, the Yales, and elsewhere." In his essay "I Love
My Country—Christ Have Mercy," he attacked blind faith in
one's government. "I believe God made the St. Lawrence River
. . . and the English Channel, but I don't believe God made
America . . . man did that." To Campbell patriotism is immoral
and a violation of the First Commandment. "Singing 'God Bless
America' in a Christian service is blasphemy," he argued. "It is
asking God to put his stamp of approval on some pretty ungodly
things. Things like taking the country away from a powerful and
friendly people . . . the rape of Mexico . . . the crushing of the
Cuban rebellion in 1898. Things like nuclear weapons which only
we have used. Things like the CIA. Things like genocide—for
where have all the redmen gone."

By 1962, Will Campbell had also become disillusioned with institutionalized race reform. Two incidents concerning the National Council of Churches led him to conclude that it was another institution designed only to sustain itself.

They happened in Albany, Georgia. The Southern Christian Leadership Conference was involved with a mass demonstration. Local officials had decreed against it. Large numbers of Northern religious leaders—rabbis, priests, and Protestant clergymen—had planned to come down to protest—and to be arrested. "You know," Campbell recalled, "I was never against that sort of thing, but I never took it very seriously either. That's too easy, you see. It's pretty easy to get on a plane in Boston, fly down to Georgia, get arrested for an hour, go back home, and then tell everyone at religious gatherings how involved you were in the civil rights crisis. They'd fly in a jet to Atlanta, get on an air-conditioned bus and come to Albany. Each was supposed to bring fifty dollars. Then the demonstrators would go to the Bethel Baptist Church. The organizer would take their fifty dollars, which meant they agreed to get arrested and bailed out right away."

Later Campbell wrote an article on the Albany demonstration for *The Christian Century* magazine, and immediately some of his fellow liberal clergymen criticized it. "They thought I was too sympathetic toward the local white people." Two things struck Campbell as comical in the Albany crisis. "There was this big police chief named Pritchet—a deeply religious man. A crowd of the demonstrators who had flown in would start kneeling on the street to pray and Pritchet would take off his cap and bow with them in prayer, then put his cap back on and order them to disperse. Of course they would not disperse, but would start to pray again, and Pritchet would take off his hat and pray with them again. That struck me as pretty ironic."

The other incident at Albany that drew criticism in Campbell's article happened one day when things didn't go as scheduled when the group arrived to pray and be arrested. Will Campbell's close friend, Andrew Young, was in charge of bailing out the demonstrators as soon as they were arrested. Instead, Young suggested to Campbell that they go back to their quarters and take a nap. Hours dragged by. "Andy," Campbell said, "you aren't going to bail them out tonight, are you?" Campbell remembered Young's response. "He told me that they wanted to be a part of the movement—so it wouldn't be good Southern hospitality if they didn't spend *one* night in a Southern jail. We bailed them out the next morning, and some were mad as hell. They said 'Now look, we agreed to come and be arrested, but not to stay overnight in a dirty jail with no air conditioning.' "

Campbell drew fire when his article appeared. He had referred to Chief Pritchet as a "good man." Some people thought that was being too sympathetic to "the enemy." "Hell, I began to wonder who the enemy was supposed to be."

Campbell was in the process of a long learning which would take him back in part to his roots in Amite County. It was one of gradual awareness, which began after he moved to Nashville in the 1950s. Much of Campbell's conversion to a *new* ministry— his championing of primitive Christianity, reform through personal experience, and concern for downtrodden Southern whites and blacks—came from his growing involvement in the world of country music.

Country music was not a hobby. "Sure I wanted to be a country singer—long before I decided to be a preacher. My first guitar was nothing more than a piece of wire tied to a milk safe; I would strum it and release tension on the wire to change sounds. Then when I was about twelve, my daddy traded a pig and got me a Hawaiian guitar. The trouble was, nobody in our community had ever seen one like that and I never learned to play it."

There was something about the music which reached deeply into his soul. "Sometimes I would not even admit it," he said, "back in my time of pseudosophistication. But the truth was, in 1956, when the National Council of Churches made me that job offer, that was the big reason why I wanted to set up headquarters in Nashville—because that was the focus point of country music."

Campbell did not then know how much the music would affect him. It became part of his ministry; when he moved to and fro in the civil rights struggle, or delivered a lecture at some university, the battered guitar case went along. He began to see the music as an expression of the fears and passions of the inner Southern soul. "Just listen to it, and you'll understand what a Southerner thinks," Campbell has said.

His new office in Nashville was squarely on the emerging Music Row. Most of the buildings were late-Victorian homes, many boasting the stained glass windows and garish cupolas of the gilded age. In the early 1900s, this had been a residential area for upper-class businessmen. By the 1940s, Nashville blacks moved into the area, driven from their older homes by urban expansion. Belmont did not want them either. Many white families sold their houses cheaply and moved out to suburban enclaves. The remaining population was a strange mixture—black undesirables, low-income whites living in large homes converted into boarding houses, elderly residents who did not move, Vanderbilt University students, and the incoming music industry people.

There they are together within a square mile—the high-powered academic culture of Vanderbilt, the music industry, and the nearby Southern Baptist citadel of Belmont College. The cultural polarities are evident along the sidewalks—aspiring songwriters in denim jackets, long-haired "Jesus freaks," short-haired Baptist student-ministers, sandal-clad Vanderbilt scholars, well-dressed publishers, and other varieties of Nashville humanity.

By the 1960s, a multimillion-dollar music industry was quartered there, one far from the reaches of control of the insurance executives who had established Nashville's country-music trade. In 1950, Capitol Records began moving its country-music operations there, followed by Mercury Records in 1952. Others followed suit, including RCA Victor and Columbia. Huge independent publishing operations grew along Music Row, such as

Cedarwood Publishing Company (1953) and Tree Publishing Company (1954). Branches of America's three music licensing corporations soon moved into Music Row. In 1958, Broadcast Music Incorporated (BMI) established offices there, followed by the American Society of Composers, Authors and Publishers (ASCAP) in the early 1960s. By the end of the 1960s, Music Row housed almost two-hundred-and-fifty publishing companies, ninety recording concerns, and the offices of numerous songwriters, singers, and talent agencies.

Many of these people became Campbell's friends since the first months after his small office opened in 1956. Some were major singers and writers; others were aspirants who had arrived on a bus from Alabama to walk the streets of the Belmont section. Gradually they came to trust Campbell, to appreciate the depth of his growing ministry of a primitive Christian humanity. Later, they began driving out to his farm at Mt. Juliet to seek counsel. If they married, Preacher Will Campbell got the call. If a father died in South Georgia, the telephone in the log office would ring. Would Will Campbell preside at the funeral?

In turn, Campbell learnt much from them and their music. He began to gain an awareness of the nature of the Southern soul, which was embraced in the major themes of country music. "There are only three themes to the music," Campbell said. "They are making love, drinking, and fighting." All three were metaphors for greater, troubling issues, and an awareness of them did much to change Will Campbell in the 1960s. The love and sex themes of the music are a metaphor for the polarization of Southern life: passion and guilt, inhibition and extreme sexual desire. Women are either docile, self-suffering housewives or passionate mistresses. Men exude an aura of bold assertion countered by the need for emotional support from women.

As we have seen, the opposites are old ones, rooted in a Southern pattern of thought which took shape before the Civil War. Then a combination of racial matters, hatred of the North, religion, political insecurity, regional pride, and other factors pushed the South to extremes. As Clement Eaton observed in *Freedom of Thought in the Old South*, everything forced the planter South to opposite poles. Human beings were saved or lost, free or unfree, were Southerners of chivalric demeanor or churlish Northerners. The middle ground of compromise became non-existent, as pulpits, college professorships, and the editorship of newspapers became vacant of dissenters.

The Civil War only intensified the absolutes, more so because it was an internal conflict which forced members of families to declare opposite loyalties. In the bitter Reconstruction years (and even now), the demand for fealty to unyielding positions regarding politics, race, and religion continued. The phrase "I'll take my stand" represents more than a lyric from the old minstrel melody "Dixie." Traditionally every facet of Southern life has been gripped by inflexibility, and an entire mosaic of catch phrases is the heritage of the land—white or black; "good nigras" or troublemakers; conservatives or liberals; saved with Jesus or damned to hell; short-haired patriots or long-haired traitors; America love it or leave it; get your heart in Dixie or get out, etc.

This underlying tension comes forth, as noted earlier, in the fundamentalist churches which have dominated the South for one-hundred-and-fifty years. The preachers are the moral keepers of the flock. Some creeds, such as the Southern Baptist, insist upon moral uprightness as evidence of true conversion. Others, such as the Church of Christ and the Pentecostal sects, intrude further and deny their members the simple comfort of conversion. "Faith without works is dead," their preachers intone, warning of the threat of falling from grace through moral lapses. Man is his own ethical battleground, torn between God and Satan. For a Dixie fundamentalist, Lucifer is synonymous with unleashed natural passion, while God is synonymous with the rigid code of conduct imposed by church deacons.

The tensions of these irreconcilable dichotomies engender universal guilt. The foundations of remorse heard in the music by Will Campbell are grounded in the southern soul. Even if there had been no slaveocracy, even if the planter class was aware of the difference between the preachings of Thomas Jefferson and the master-chattel relationship, there would have been guilt in the music. Certainly the Civil War and the awareness of failing the American dream nourished the feeling. More importantly, this guilt came from the mother earth of Southern piety, of the tradition that man is good but also evil, one who strives to overcome but often fails. The entire rich fabric of Dixie's literature and music is grounded in a credo that man is fallible.

The music Campbell heard—and still plays often—was an admission of this frailty. Somehow everyone feels guilty in a country song, as one is caught between the institutions of one's heritage and natural passions. In the stark lyrics of "Putting On the Midnight Oil," a female singer describes an afterhour liaison at the office, bemoaning the fact that she would "be sorry." In fact, guilt is so pervasive in the music that thought constitutes sin no less than desire. In "Almost Persuaded," a male singer laments a near-rendezvous with a temptress. Although he resisted, he nevertheless felt remorse from having the desire.

Love relationships rarely end well in country music. Will Campbell sings such melodies as "Heartaches by the Number," "Making Believe That You Still Love Me," or "I'm So Lonesome I Could Cry." It is a music of division and remorse. Lovers die young, romances are broken by unhappiness, marriages fail, or illicit relationships produce shame.

The attitudes of guilt and pessimism were present in the traditional British ballads brought into the Southern Appalachians in the eighteenth century. In the homeland, the British melodies encompassed a broad range of topics. In the Southern highlands, those which survived the trek to the New World were mainly melodies of tragic love.

In 1916, the Englishman Cecil Sharp came to the Southern mountains to work on a famous compendium of British songs in the Appalachians. In eastern Tennessee, the first song Sharp encountered was an old British tune, "The Gypsy Laddie." Change the time period, add a steel guitar and one would have the elements of a modern country song. It told of a wife who ran away with a lover only to experience guilt and disgrace.

Such ballads include all the contradictions which underscore modern country-music's view of love and sex: it is one of half sexual fantasy and half morality play. Lust and guilt, sensuality and sin, were, say the ballad experts, what mountain people longed to hear. They were products of a drive for escapism— tunes of revenge against lovers, sexual fantasy, and guilt.

The social disruption and new mobility in the South produced by the Civil War only intensified the message. A culture long wedded to family and locale was shaken by a new realism. Love and passion never ended well because the rigors of society would not allow it. By the early 1960s, when Campbell still maintained his office on Music Row, over fifty percent of all country music dealt with infidelity and its unhappy aftermath, e.g., Hank Williams's "Your Cheating Heart," or "Ruby, Don't Take Your Love to Town," a painful lament of a bedridden Vietnam veteran who could no longer perform for a restless young wife. "They were Jesus sounds, too," Campbell recalled later. They were fantasy, cloaked in direct themes and lyrics which were often stark if not crude.

Will Campbell's first book, *Race and the Renewal of the Church*, in 1962, was a radical piece of literature for a man accustomed to moving within liberal reform circles, one who received hate mail and veiled threats of violence from Deep South segregationists. It was also radical for one who had labored, since 1956, within the institutional confines of the National Council of Churches.

In this book, Campbell asserted that formal religious organizations had *failed* in the civil rights crisis. This was the first declaration of his new calling: to appeal to one's personal Christian conscience to lift up the blacks, the condemned prisoner, or the Ku Klux Klansman. In Campbell's opinion, it would have been better had the Supreme Court not ruled favorably on the race issue in 1954. The matter would then have been left squarely to the individual Christian to resolve. Christians would have been forced to say, "Thus saith the Lord! Not, Thus saith the law!" It was radical as well, because Will Campbell, who had stood at Little Rock, on the streets of Montgomery, and elsewhere, suggested that the church should care for the segregationist. The church "must love and redeem him. It must somehow set him free."

Even Campbell himself was not yet free. He would learn a second crucial lesson about the Southern soul and about himself: one could become alienated from one's roots. His teachers were his brother Joe and a Mississippi radical newspaper editor named P. D. East. For a time, East had published a small newspaper, *The Petal Paper*, which poked fun at the White Citizens' Councils, prominent segregationist politicians, and others. After many threats upon his life, East moved to the community of Fairhope, Alabama, outside of urban Mobile, where he eked out a living through small grants obtained for him by prominent Southern liberal spokesmen.

One day in the middle 1960s, Campbell arrived at East's home to visit with his brother Joe and the wandering editor. "There I was, sitting with two of the most troubled men I had ever seen, and they were teaching me."

The lesson centered upon the death of Jonathan Daniel, a friend of Campbell's. Daniel, a student from the Episcopal Theological Seminary in Cambridge, Massachusetts, had been working for black voter-registration in the segregationist region of Lowndes County, Alabama. While doing this, Daniel and a Roman Catholic priest from Chicago had been arrested and held for a few days in the county jail at Hayneville. On the day they were released, the men had stopped with two black students at a small grocery store on the edge of town to purchase soft drinks. The proprietress, alarmed at the mixed group, telephoned a special deputy named Thomas Coleman. Coleman arrived as Daniel and the priest were leaving the premises, and opened fire with a shotgun. Daniel fell dead at the first shot; then the deputy turned and fired at the priest, who fell mortally wounded.

Will Campbell heard the news in P. D. East's home. Angrily he began condemning red-necks in the South, the breakdown of law and order, and the entire population of Dixie who were little more than "Kluxers," crackers, and ignoramuses. Then East brought him to a new awareness with a simple question: "Now Brother, let's see if your definition of the faith can stand the test. Was Jonathan Daniel a bastard?"

Once before, in an earlier conversation, while driving on a lonely Mississippi road, East had demanded from Campbell a definition of the Christian faith "in ten words or less." Campbell had shot back, "We're all bastards, but God loves us anyway."

Now East's voice rose higher until he almost yelled, "So tell me *now!* Was Jonathan Daniel a bastard?"

"Yes," Campbell said.

"Well," East continued, "was that deputy, Thomas Coleman, a bastard?"

Campbell thought that one was easier to resolve. "Yes—Thomas Coleman is a bastard."

East now drove home his point, one which Will Campbell will never forget. He pulled his chair closer and stared intently at Campbell. "So Jonathan Daniel *was* a bastard and Thomas Coleman *is* a bastard. So tell me now, which one of those bastards do you think God loves the most?"

Campbell began to shake, choked up for a moment, and then burst into tears. Then he started laughing. "I was laughing at myself, at being for twenty years in a ministry of liberal sophistication, and worshipping at shrines of enlightenment and academia, of human engineering, and dictates of the Supreme Court, theology, law, and order. I had denied not only the faith I was supposed to hold, but had denied, as well, my history and my people. My people were the Thomas Colemans, too, with their shotguns. Loved by God. And if loved, forgiven, and if forgiven, reconciled."

Campbell later saw the incident as one in which he was led to come to terms with his own alienation from a heritage. "Like a lot of Southern liberals, I had tried to deny my own history—to run from it, and to insulate myself in activist movements, education, and sophistication, so I could pretend I had never lived in East Fork.

"It was that day in P. D. East's house," Campbell recalled later, "that I really understood for the first time the nature of tragedy, and those who realize the nature of tragedy cannot take sides. I had taken sides. Had left East Fork and had become a little arrogant in my new liberation and learning. I justified my alienation from Amite County by finding excitement in the civil rights movement. I even learned to say 'redneck' in the same ugly tones that others say 'nigger.' "

For Campbell now, the real understanding of tragedy was to realize that he had picked the wrong enemy. Later, in a speech to the Southern Regional Council, he asserted his new faith: that the Southern poor whites he had once railed against were victims also, were casualties of institutions which had enslaved them. His speech was an affirmation of the lesson learned from P. D. East that day. Campbell said, "One of the mistakes we made was to take sides. We took sides because we did not really understand the nature of the tragedy. We, who were white and who liked to see ourselves as liberal, whether we were in fact or not, thought we understood the suffering and injustices black people had had heaped upon them. We really *didn't* understand, but took sides anyway. We left home, proud of our sophistication, and joined the movement. We marched across the Selma bridge, or walked to school in Little Rock or New Orleans with a few black children as we should have done. We learned to cuss Mississippi sheriffs and to use the term 'redneck.' "

Campbell argued now that perhaps the "redneck" was the greatest sufferer, trapped in a web of alienation from himself and his heritage. For the poor whites "had their heads taken away by the cunning, skillful, and well-educated gentlemen of the upper-class," who told them their economic and political weakness was a fault of black people. "So the 'redneck' picked the wrong enemy. He never knew, and still doesn't know, that black people are not what he has to fight if he is ever going to remedy his own plight." The enemy of the black militant and the Klansman was the same. The enemy was the institution—the political, economic, and religious forces which divided people and separated them from the realization of a simple faith in Campbell's own ten-word definition of Christianity: "We are all bastards, but God loves us anyway."

In 1978, Campbell appeared at a symposium, "Mississippi: Sense of Place," at the University of Southern Mississippi. Several prominent writers and educators who shared a common heritage had gathered to discuss what it had meant to grow up in the paradoxical climate of love and hate. Will Campbell's talk, "Staying Home or Leaving," attempted to verbalize his own love-hate relationship with the region. It was an admission of something learned that day at the feet of P. D. East—the awareness that alienation is intrinsic to the Southern soul.

P. D. East was not the only one who taught Campbell that all Southern folk—black and white—are shrouded in alienation. The music in Nashville taught him the same lesson. That day at Southern Mississippi, Will Campbell's lecture pivoted upon the outpouring of the soul in country music. He was unable to define what a sense of place was, or to verbalize what alienation was. Instead, he returned to the music, and read lyrics by writers and singers who had grown up in Mississippi. There was "Throw a Rope Around the Wind," written by his friend Red Lane, who had grown up in the tough Poplarville community of the sandy pine belt. To Lane, attempting to find a reason for staying home or leaving was as difficult as finding a raindrop in the sand.

Campbell then turned to the song "Mississippi, You're On My Mind." It was written by a native, Jesse Winchester, who had departed for Canada during the days of the Vietnam draft. Stoney Edwards, a black singer, had recorded the song which told of an unattractive land, with hungry dogs everywhere, snakes sleeping in thick weeds, and tar-paper shacks lining gaunt wagon roads filled with emptiness. Still, in the chorus, the singer admitted that Mississippi was forever on his mind.

Will Campbell then turned to the lyrics of a song which had been recorded by another black singer, Charley Pride, who grew up in Sledge, Mississippi. The song seemed to speak of nostalgia, of how the singer was awakened by the crowing of a rooster to view the verdant, pastoral scenes of fields heavy with dew and dotted with fat lazy cows. But in the last line, the singer repeated the song title, "But I Wonder Could I Live There Anymore?" It was only a nice place to think about and even to visit.

The irony was that even though the musicians attempted to sever ties with their Southern heritage, the old religious, rural, and blue-collar traditions could not be shaken off. Most of them, particularly in Nashville, had undergone a long orientation in Southern fundamentalist religion. The debt to religious heritage was immense. They had learned the old three-chord Southern hymns which still dominate country melodies. Singer Dolly Parton's melody of infidelity, "It's All Wrong But It's All Right" contains the same chord patterns as did the revival tunes she sang in her grandfather's holiness church in the Great Smoky Mountains. In addition, these religious roots provided many themes basic to the music—contrasts between right and wrong, guilt, the polarization of humankind into well-defined categories of saint and sinner.

Often the Nashville musician makes war against the religion and community which nurtured the talent. Nashville offers America a neat, commercialized image of country music. Television presents images of haystacks, rocking chairs, and heavy doses of rural downhome jargon. Here is one of the great Southern ironies which Will Campbell observed on Music Row. Onstage, performers act out a life which, in private, they strive to reject. Most agree with the famous songwriter Bob McDill's observation that "I would never go back to where I was, to being a nobody, being powerless and helpless." The alternative is to do something which the Southern soul is incapable of achieving—to make a break with one's past. In time, Will Campbell learned this lesson and now ministers to country musicians who failed also to make the break, but yet have tried to sever enough times to find themselves almost rootless. They desperately attempt to reject the old world. Yet they are not free of it at all.

Instead, many live in large Nashville castles, amid an aura of estrangement and isolation. Some of the isolation is understandable. Singers are besieged by adoring fans while on road trips. Some admirers try to enter their motel rooms, private buses, or backstage dressing rooms. Others bring pies and cakes to concerts and press them on the band.

But even after road trips, singers find little escape from adulation. Nashville newsstands peddle maps of "the homes of the stars." The tour buses are ready on weekends to take visitors out along the Granny White Pike to Eddy Arnold's place or over on the Franklin Pike to Tammy Wynette's mansion. The buses stop at Johnny Cash's home out on Old Hickory Lake and the tourists emerge and lean across the fence to snap pictures. Out in Brentwood, they peer through the big redwood fence surrounding Waylon Jennings's home. Somebody pulls up a sprig of grass to take home and press between the pages of the family Bible. On weekends, Nashville is bedlam for a singer who seeks privacy.

But the need for privacy does not explain totally the alienation one senses along Music Row, because the garrison mentality is not confined to stars. One observes it among writers, publishers, record producers, sidemen, and everyone else in Nashville who has some financial interest in the guitar.

Some of the most secluded people never have to worry about privacy, because they are virtually unknown. They are the hundreds of people hanging on in Nashville, hoping for recognition, and the several thousand country musicians out in the Southern hinterlands who dream of a career on Music Row. If one observes any fifth-rate country musician in any Southern locale one will have a composite of the isolation syndrome which pervades the entire hillbilly music industry. The performer will have his own inner circle of cronies and groupies. He will grant interviews, but the responses will be so vague and general that the questioner will marvel how such expressive music can come from such an inarticulate person. The local singer will boast an unlisted telephone number and a record of having lived in half-a-dozen residences within the past year. Even in a small Dixie hamlet, a singer will possess lavish business cards. Often, the printed address is crossed out and a new one handwritten in.

Whether a musician lives in Nashville or in South Georgia, the sociology does not change. He is caught in an isolated, fluid world which demands public notice and anonymity at the same time. Nashville is the mecca where if the dream materializes, the life-style remains the same.

It is one of the great ironies of the South and of its music. The lyrics may be earthy and direct, but the writers and singers are alienated from their soil and heritage.

Modern Nashville, Will Campbell's parish, provides the symbols of alienation, both past and present. The symbols of the Old Confederacy are still present as reminders of separatism: The statue of Sam David, the "Boy Hero of the Confederacy," rests on the state-capital grounds; the spire of the Downtown Presbyterian Church, where wounded federal soldiers were treated in 1864; Belle Meade mansion, where rebel officers were quartered; and the rows of metal battlefield markers stretching out to Franklin along the old roads. The modern symbolism is more pervasive. If a songwriter or singer requires the inspiration of a feeling of estrangement, Nashville is the ideal setting. It juxtaposes the creative culture of country music against the no-nonsense business-religious ethos which controls the city.

Sometimes Will Campbell takes his guitar and delivers the message of singer Tom T. Hall's song "Homecoming," an autobiography of the musician's own upbringing in Kentucky. The pale, gaunt singer is on the road and stops to talk with his rural father. The old world has vanished, but is there still to trouble the entertainer. No one is comfortable, particularly the singer with his gaudy costume jewelry. He is off somewhere in a world in between where he is supposed to be and where he once lived.

Campbell is singing the exaggeration of his own life—of someone trapped between two worlds. He understands the torment of the Nashville musician. The memory of a rancid greasepit of a Georgia service station is still real enough, and the musician constantly fears that he might return there. He does not want to go home, yet is unable to free himself from the old bonds of family, home, and community. Will Campbell's message to the singer is the same he learned that day at the home of P. D. East. Accept one's situation and be reconciled, because we are all bastards whom God loves.

The music helped to teach Will Campbell a third lesson of the Southern soul. In the triad of themes of country music, there is also *violence*. Violence swirled around Will Campbell in his labors for the National Council of Churches. Clad in his wrinkled suit and black preacher's hat, Campbell moved in and out of trouble spots.

He witnessed, first hand, brutality, fear, anger, and physical force. In 1956, on the streets of the small mountain community of Anderson, Tennessee, were crowds of dispossessed poor whites, fearful of the coming desegregation which had been decreed in a Knoxville court. Cars were overturned, the school was dynamited, and black children were threatened. "I was there talking to this local Baptist preacher," Campbell recalled. "A few days later he fell in with some black children walking up the hill to the school. A white mob grabbed him and beat him severely. I remember thinking about what I had told my brother Joe, that 'They don't kill white people in Mississippi.' Now I knew things had changed."

Campbell felt the surge of the white mob and withstood the taunts and threats in 1957 as he escorted black children to Central High School in Little Rock. "It was pretty explosive," he remembers. "I was at a meeting at the Dunbar Community Center with some of the black parents and children. The father of a fifteen-year-old girl—he was a quiet, gentle man, I remember—said 'Mr. Campbell, I've seen black people killed before in Arkansas by white men. I am not a violent person, but I am armed, and if anybody harms my baby, I will kill them.' A lot of black and white people were armed, and I began to wonder what would happen when those nine children walked the several blocks to the high school. Now I don't claim to be a hero, but what does it mean to be a *real* human being in such a situation? So four of us just fell in and walked through the big mob with the children."

Campbell's labors took him through many such mobs, through police dogs, clubs, tear gas, and bleeding demonstrators. He came to Montgomery in 1961, when angry mobs attacked busloads of "Freedom Riders" who were sponsored by the Congress of Racial Equality. The next year he was in Birmingham, when police used firehoses and dogs to combat demonstrators, and went back later that year when four small black children were killed in a bomb explosion at the Sixteenth Street Baptist Church. Meanwhile, he journeyed to the University of Mississippi in the wake of the riots over the admission of James Meredith—riots which left two men dead—and visited with the new student. He was in Nashville and Greensboro during the fury of lunch-counter demonstrations, and saw violence again on the march from Selma to Montgomery. And Campbell was present in the long train at Atlanta, to bury his friend and brother, Martin Luther King, Jr.

There was a singular incident in the long nightmare which indicated the change of direction occurring in Will Campbell's ministry. In 1966, James Meredith was shot as he walked along a Mississippi highway. Campbell and other clergymen went to Meredith's bedside to give comfort. Only Will Campbell left the hospital to minister to the man who had shot Meredith.

It was an early foray into the new ministry destined to encompass life in the hollow at Mt. Juliet. Part of Will Campbell's understanding of those he had considered *the enemy* in earlier years, the downtrodden Southern poor whites, came from the teaching of country music. Already the music had taught him how all Southerners were polarized and alienated. It also gave him a deeper understanding of the years of suffering he had seen in the civil rights crisis.

Violence appears intrinsic to the Southern soul, and the sheer mention of it can produce a host of images. Violence was General Andrew Jackson destroying the Creek Indian nation at the battle of Horseshoe Bend; the code *duello* in antebellum Louisiana; General "Stonewall" Jackson's apology to his wife for making war on the Protestant Sabbath; ex-rebel General Nathan Bedford Forrest leading white-robed comrades of the Knights of the Invisible Empire; the brutal Appalachian Mountain feuds; the Harlan, Kentucky labor wars, lynchings; the Scottsboro boys; and the murders in Philadelphia, Mississippi.

For decades, historians and sociologists have sought to explain the roots of the South's violent spirit. Some point to the region's isolation; the frontier did last longer in Dixie. The Creek Indian confederacy resisted with force until the decade 1830–40, while river and land pirates combed isolated Dixie roads. Other observers have pointed to the cotton kingdom in the era before the Civil War. Southern romanticism, with its chivalric subcults of the defense of honor and proficiency with weapons, did create a paramilitary society. Besides, by the outbreak of the Civil War, the planter class held over three-and-a-half million people in bondage—itself an act of violence.

Others point to the Civil War and its aftermath. Over 618,000 Americans perished in the conflict—more than were killed in all other American efforts from the Revolution to the end of the Korean conflict in the 1950s. One of every three *rebel* soldiers perished, as did one of every nineteen white Southerners. The end of the war only brought more violence. The war engendered a century of racial conflict. It also spawned decades of anger about poverty and illiteracy experienced by both white and black alike. Will Campbell came to understand, however, that this definition of Southern violence was too limited. The dictionary provided a more appropriate description. Violence is more than manslaughter or assault. It is passion, strong feeling, and an adulation of physical force.

All this is central to the Southern soul—and its music. Dixie has a cult of the physical, is a passionate land which for generations has idolized force and power. In effect, violence takes many forms. It is in the football popularity of a Paul "Bear" Bryant or the adoration showered upon NASCAR race-car drivers on the Southern circuit. It becomes the tan-legged Tigerbelle twirlers of Louisiana State University or the adoration for a local football coach in a Southern hamlet. Violence can be the proverbial Good Ole Boy with his gentle disdain for the law. It is assertive male talk at a roadside tavern, beauty contestants trained since puberty like thoroughbred horses, or the admiration for gusto in political oratory. It is an idolatry of bigness, strength, force, extremism, and a mild disrespect for authority.

Both types of violence—genuine physical harm and the admiration for things physical—are deeply imbedded in country music, and have been since the beginning. The British Child ballads, which breathed life into Campbell's religious music, were violent, brooding, and pessimistic. Topics covered homicide, broken-hearted lovers, deaths of sweethearts or children, murder-suicide pacts, and other tragic events. The hero in "Lord Randal" is poisoned by his sweetheart; the "Cruel Mother" kills her illegitimate children with a penknife; and in "Fair Margaret and Sweet William," the spurned female commits suicide and William dies of remorse.

Native American folk tunes of the nineteenth century, which also found their way into Will Campbell's melodies, repeated the theme of violence. Folk tunes such as "Banks of the Ohio" and "Knoxville Girl" provided sadistic accounts of the murder of women, while "I Will Never Marry" told of a rejected lover's suicide. Violence and unhappiness permeated the early commercial country music heard by Will Campbell in his East Fork home. A mother died in "Will the Circle Be Unbroken," while a child dies in his sleep in "Don't Make Me Go to Bed and I'll Be Good." In the 1950s and later, Campbell heard the same themes of physical harm, death, or hostility on Nashville's streets. A man prepares to kill his unfaithful sweetheart in "Laura"; a disloyal wife is murdered in "The Cold Hard Facts of Life"; while in "El Paso," the tragic hero is riddled with bullets when he attempts a rendezvous with the woman he loves.

There is a second, and far deeper, level of violence in the South and its music. Spiritual or moral death is endemic to Southern culture. The late James McBride Dabbs, for a long time president of the Southern Regional Council, described the Southerner's awareness of tragedy: it is the resolution of a Stoic conviction that life is expected to be brief and unsatisfying and, as a result, tragic. For every song of physical death, there are scores which tell of the destruction of the soul. At least seventy-five percent of the successful melodies which reach the national charts are concerned with the annihilation of a marriage or love affair. It is an intermingling of the themes of tragic separation, the disruption of the home, and consequent moral decay.

The music Will Campbell heard in Nashville possessed a third and still deeper level. More important than actual violence was sheer physical assertion. If religion has a rival for dominance of the Southern soul, it is the credo of potential physical action, and the admiration for those who exist in the gray area between order and rebellion. This can be the most frightening aspect of Southern culture, more fearsome even than the threats of real crime. Always there is the subtle threat of manslaughter or mere physical force; the implication is always there that someone is prepared to become his own law.

Campbell realized more and more what produced much of this obsession with the physical and powerful. There is *too* much bravado in Dixie and its music, too much bluster and reinforcement of the male ego. Violence is an exercise of power. The admiration of power is an old Southern trait which dates back to the cotton kingdom of the early nineteenth century. The rise of the cotton empire before the Civil War was an exercise in violence and power. The would-be planters swarmed onto the new kingdom stretching from Georgia to Texas. Hundreds of thousands of black people were bought and sold as cattle, were wrenched from their homes on the Atlantic seaboard, and forced into the heat and loneliness of the Deep South. Cotton was white gold, and planters kept grabbing more land. They leveled forests, drained swamps, and built levees to hold back the Yazoo swamps.

Many of the cotton planters were self-made men, the nouveaux riches. In the older South they had been middle-class
farmers, younger sons with no hope of inheritance, or worse,
plantation overseers despised even by their fellow whites. Now
they had power and money and sought to prove it—perhaps to
themselves. Lavish homes were built, and an entire code of chiv-
alry was fashioned. Planters' sons were schooled in the several
cults of the chivalric ideal—defend your honor, idolize your
women, and be skilled in the arts of manhood, weapons and
horsemanship. It was all the shaping of a self-image. Cotton
farming was a fickle business where financial calamity threatened
with every drought, heavy rain, or whim of a Northern agent.
Power was an immediate thing and proof it demanded a showy
presence, which masked insecurity.

One suspects that the Civil War only intensified the insecurity. Defeat blasted Southern belief in their superior martial arts
and physical prowess. Appomattox may have been an almost
psychological emasculation of Southern males reared in a land
which had canonized virility, strength, and proficiency with
weapons. Lee's surrender was the beginning of an enduring rationale for defeatism.

The rationale has involved a reassertion of the cult of male
power. The old pre-Civil War cult of firearms and horsemanship
became NASCAR racing, Alabama football, and Huey Long.
The rationale has involved an endless chain of power displays:
the adoration of contact sports; the montage of pickup trucks and
gunracks; automobile bumper stickers which suggest physical
threats against political dissenters. It is found in the bravado of
young insurance executives and their wives in football stadium
parking lots, touting flasks of bourbon; the lusty talk in a highway truckstop when an attractive woman passes. The only difference between the button-down junior executive in the parking
lot and the oglers at the diner is style.

Nowhere is this ambivalence of power and insecurity more
apparent than in the image of the "Good Ole Boy." In the real
sense, he is almost an economic composite of blue-collar, small-

town Southern existence. He is the gasoline station employee whose blue pickup truck boasts a tapedeck playing the latest offerings from Merle Haggard. Good Ole Boys are churchgoers, who espouse some Baptist or Church of Christ doctrine given forth in a drab, sweat-filled, frame-church building. And in terms of the basic Southern paradox, their attitudes toward the Almighty are ambivalent. Attending church is a social occasion, providing an opportunity to perch on a dusty carhood and discuss carburetors. Yet beneath their discomfort at wearing a white shirt on Sunday, there rests a basic sin-obsessed Calvinism. Religion is a dark, personal matter. They never discuss their religious faith. Still, they turn out in large numbers for annual religious revivals, where many of them are "born again."

The politics of the Good Ole Boy are almost as guarded as his religion. Here one senses a holdover from that pre-Civil War chivalric mentality—a fierce pride in one's politics and respect for differences in that of a neighbor's. Good Ole Boys never discuss their politics. Instead, they spend much time in such places as gasoline stations and barber shops, talking politics in the abstract. Their frequent themes are right-wing conservatism, dislike of liberals, and a love for the American military. They are the people who boosted Merle Haggard to stardom in the early 1960s. Haggard's songs, such as "Okie from Muskogee," "The Fighting Side of Me," and "I Take a Lot of Pride in What I Am" symbolized their political faith.

Ironically, these same Good Ole Boys in large part prepared the country-music world for the acceptance of black artist Charley Pride. Just as Haggard sang their politics, Pride expressed their concept of the good Southern life—home, mamma, family, and the rural ways. Pride's songs embody their social aspirations. His lyrics boast of the tranquility of rural life and how it is superior to that of the city. Above all, Pride's music embodies that Good Ole Boy concept that what is important is not doing, but being. Songs such as "All I Have to Offer You Is Me" emphasize a reverse pride in being Southern, rural, and poor. In Charley Pride's music, the Good Ole Boy finds the praise of men close to the land, the decency of rural America.

The insecurity which haunts the Southerner pervades his music—and conversely. On the surface, Nashville's music is an image of masculine boldness, physical assertion, and power. Underneath, it is the music of a dispossessed class, and, as Will Campbell came to understand, lost souls as well. Some were mill workers in the Carolina textile plants who had labored since they were fifteen for low wages amid shabby conditions. They were tenant farmers or the sons of tenant farmers—as was Will Campbell—who grew up in a modern feudal fiefdom. Some were small farmers driven from the land by economic forces beyond their control; now they worked in Birmingham steel mills, and were trapped somewhere between their rural Baptist values and a new social order. They were residents of small Southern towns, alien to the greater social changes affecting America, and fearful of rights for black people whom they had been taught to hate.

Steadily, through the admonitions of P. D. East and the words of his brother Joe, the image of an Albany police chief with bowed head, and the music itself, Campbell was coming to realize, by the early 1960s, that *these* people were also the downtrodden. The music—if not the lives of the country singers to whom Campbell ministered—provided only exaggerations of the frustrations of millions of Southern noninheritors.

There was no one to speak for them save the musicians and an occasional Will Campbell. They had been polarized by institutions. Churches had driven them to extremes of right and wrong, while the political and social order had divided them from their neighboring poor blacks. Another institution, the government, had sent them to Vietnam, and had divided them against those who would not serve for reasons of conscience. So they went to Southeast Asia, from Georgia mobile homes and Mississippi cotton farms. Fewer returned, only to find that the nation still scorned them as "red-necks," belittled their primitive fundamentalist religions, and mocked their culture in the entertainment media.

Institutions also did much to instill the sense of alienation already imbedded in their Southern souls. The political and economic power structure of the planter class had led them to war in 1861, telling them that the North was *the* enemy of their culture. Three-fourths of these people did not own slaves, but hundreds of thousands still perished or suffered horrible wounds. Later, caught in the grip of abject poverty in the decades after Appomattox, the institutions told them once again there were aliens to fight. The black man was their enemy said the power structure. Do not unify all poor Southern folk. Unite Southern whites against black people who somehow are responsible for three-cent cotton, pitiful schools, and hookworm. Meanwhile, the growing power of the Southern Baptist faith and other fundamentalist institutions preached that the world itself was alien. Loving humankind was unimportant, nor was the church concerned about the cough of a textile worker, or the lack of bathrooms at a black Arkansas school. The only valid concerns are salvation or damnation, good and evil.

Thus, there is no mystery to the elements of violence, passion, and physical bravado which are part of the soul of the South and its music—a music of pride injured although it is never surrendered, of defiance admitted, and of insecurities submerged.

Will Campbell had come to lecture at an Eastern divinity school. He had with him a few notes, the guitar case, and a list of songs. The preaching was found more in the music than in the oratory, and the melodies were from the broader context of violence in the Southern spirit. "Mamma's Hungry Eyes" told of life on a starving tenant farm. "There Goes My Everything" spoke of moral failure in a broken love affair. "Mamma Bake a Pie, Daddy Kill a Chicken" spoke of the return to the Deep South of a Vietnam veteran who had lost a limb. "Catfish John" related the trials of a white Mississippi boy who was forbidden from fishing on the riverbank with an ex-slave. The final song was "Old Dogs, Children and Watermelon Wine." It was a ballad of the revelation of some truths learned from an aged black janitor late at night in a Miami barroom. The old man spoke of life in the South, of the need to bring people back together again by a common humanity which could have faith in things such as a small child or dog.

Will Campbell was discovering his own people. "You know, one thing I began to realize in the early sixties was that one vital aspect of being a human being is to come to terms with your own history, whatever it is. I learned the lesson from a lot of things. Even learned it from some black militants like Stokeley Carmichael and Rap Brown. There came a time when they said, 'Look Will, we think we have our own people pretty well under control now, and maybe you should go home and work with your own people.' I told them, 'Why man, I don't know if I can do that. My people are Kluxers and crackers and rednecks. They'd kill me.' Well, Stokeley allowed that he had been familiar with that for some time, but that he still thought it would be best if I went on back to the house."

Back to the house . . . to the beginning of a new awareness of his roots and the message in his people's music. "I began learning something about my own history. I found out that part of it was not as ugly as I had thought it was and part of it was a whole lot worse. And I found some idols that I had tripped over and busted my tail on without even knowing I had stumbled."

The year was 1963. Leaders of major religious faiths had convened a massive Centennial Conference on Religion and Race in Chicago—exactly one hundred years after President Abraham Lincoln had signed the Emancipation Proclamation. "But somebody on the planning committee didn't want to be reminded of slavery," Campbell said. So it was named the National Conference on Religion and Race. "It was supposed to be the conference to end all conferences," Campbell recalled. Martin Luther King, Jr. would speak, as would Sargent Shriver, then Director of the Peace Corps and Rabbi Abraham Heschel, the militant opponent of the Vietnam War. Will Campbell was also scheduled to address the thousands who had gathered for the conference. "That speech was a turning point in my life," Campbell admits.

The conference officials had requested that each speaker furnish a copy of his speech in advance, since the proceedings were to be published. In his prepared text, Campbell had stated that racism is a two-edged sword, that if people are equal, black and white, they must accept the fact that all men are at once good and evil. So, the text intoned, "if I live to be as old as my father is now, I expect to see black people killing white people for the same reason that white people have killed black people."

"I was only trying to make a point about equality," Campbell remembered. "If blacks were equally good, they are equally bad or they are not equal at all."

The same paragraph contained other material which disturbed the conference officials. "I was trying to make the audience see that the race problem was not something that was happening just in the United States, but was a worldwide issue. After all, two-thirds of the world's people—and all of the emerging nations—are nonwhite. So because racism is not something just reserved for white people, I suggested in the offensive paragraph that 'with the emerging powers being primarily of the darker races, I expect to see little white children marched into the gas chambers, clutching their little dolls to their breasts in Auschwitz fashion at the hands of black Eichmanns."

Two days before the convention opened, its officials began to pressure him. "Man, you can't say that," one argued. "Well that's what I believe," Campbell retorted. "Well, believe it back in Tennessee, but don't say it in Chicago!" So he didn't. In the large press gallery, reporters were taking bets on whether Campbell would deliver the infamous paragraph, while executives of the National Council of Churches wrung their hands in despair. When Campbell reached the statement in his text, he simply stood in a moment of silence and watched as the national press read the lines which he had omitted.

The media concentrated on the lines Campbell had omitted. "I think *Time* magazine mentioned only the paragraph I left out and ignored everything else." Back home in Mississippi, in the other camp, the newspapers ignored the infamous paragraph and concentrated on what Will Campbell had said. Larger newspapers and local press boasted headlines warning how LOCAL MAN ADVOCATES RACIAL MIXING and AMITE COUNTY NATIVE CALLS FOR OPEN HOUSING.

Meanwhile, Campbell's superiors in the National Council of Churches called him in. From now on, they suggested, it would be best if Campbell would submit all of his major speeches and articles for approval. Campbell asked why. "Some official cleared his throat and told me, 'Well, just to make sure we're not playing into the hands of the enemy.' " "I told them that in all the time I was in Mississippi, they may have put human feces in my punch but they never asked to see a speech I was going to make. And I was not going to do it for the supposedly most enlightened, liberal organization in the country." Will Campbell had no more enemies. He resigned his position.

EVENING

Campbell knows all about agony and human suffering of the South. Robert Penn Warren has described his book *Brother to a Dragonfly* as "fascinating and important." It is a chronicle of joy and anguish of a Mississippi upbringing in a South which has been a constant battleground between God and the devil.

Campbell came out of a Mississippi of the Depression years which resembled far more the days of Jefferson Davis than the modern South. Mississippi has always exhibited the exaggerated side of those Southern contradictions which have brought about a love-hate relationship of its people to the South. Mississippi has always been associated with an incredible dark beauty and a drab loneliness. Its world is one of charming mansions in Natchez, a dismal land of sagging tenant shacks, outdoor privies, and rusty automobiles in frontyards.

The Southern contradictions which produced a Will Campbell involved more than just the natural setting. It was almost as if God and the devil made a pact to have their struggle in Mississippi. Small-town Good Ole Boys on country store porches made easy talk—but easy talk could lead eventually to manslaughter. God was alive and well in scores of rural Baptist churches, but Satan dominated in the forms of guilt, brooding, sensuality, mental illness, sexual exaggeration, self-doubt, and that ever-present Southern loneliness.

Always there was that presence of the physical nature of the land. *Brother to a Dragonfly* is a saga of Campbell and his brother Joe, who grew up in the South of Hoover and Roosevelt. Jules Feiffer observed that the chapters on childhood days evoked Mark Twain; certainly they may be the best description of life in the rural South during the Depression years. Here again is the great contradiction. The Southern Renascence was in full bloom for Mississippians such as William Faulkner and Eudora Welty. Will Campbell's world was miles away from Oxford society. It was East Fork in the dirt poor years, when he and his brother Joe were too poor to purchase four-cent school lunches. It was a world of sawbriers on a dismal country road, the scent of flowers at a vivid country funeral, the stench of hog pens on a July day, and the fearful pounding of wind and rain on a tin roof.

Always Joe was the assumed leader and protector of the more shy and sensitive Will; he was the fighter of battles and maker of decisions. Actually, he was not stronger, because he did not recognize that part of strength is to acknowledge one's frailty. Southern manhood never admitted this, although the suspicion of it lurks beneath the surface. Too wedded to the Puritan ethic that success is a sign of Jehovah's grace, too fearful of violating the chivalric code garnered from the words of Sir Walter Scott and other romantics, Joe and his peers sought success, for failure would mean impotence.

The Second World War came, and was the turning point for Joe. He was never the same after it, being unable to fathom an outside world whose regimentation stifled his exuberance. Like Stephen Vincent Benét's Robert E. Lee, he wanted *something*. His *something* should have meant an acknowledgment of the fact that the South was a land of contrast of good and evil, strength and frailty.

Perhaps he realized this—at least he did later. But he could not cope, and transferred his aggressions into a burning desire to overcome his poor rural background, to never again be embarrassed by eating country ham and corn bread at school while wealthier children devoured baloney sandwiches. His behavior of exuberance and wild spending began, and, being a druggist, he supported it with endless pills. Then after the tragedy of a broken marriage, debts, and other unkept promises, Joe died of a massive heart attack.

Some clucked their tongues at Joe, and asserted that brother Will had taken the more honorable path. After all, his ordination as a Baptist minister was followed by years of college and post-graduate training. Then Will became a courageous fighter in the civil rights crisis of the 1960s in lower Dixie. He knew the smell of a Mississippi jail, the sweat of Georgia courtrooms in summer, and the oppressive fear of the unknown on a sultry Alabama night. For his distinguished work in the National Council of Churches and his part in the struggle for the rights of Southern blacks, Campbell was marked by old friends and fellow church-men as an Ishmael, a troublemaker—and certainly a wild-eyed liberal.

Yet were the paths of the two brothers so different? Gradually Will Campbell came to understand that the good in Southern culture was not easily defined. Once Joe angrily defended his use of drugs by accusing his brother of depending upon another op-iate—the civil rights crisis—to see him through the problems of Southern life.

Joe's remarks at first did not strike home, but eventually they made an impression on his brother. Will realized that his ener-gies had been expended in defending only one dispossessed group. What of lower-income Southern whites, hooted at in network television comedies and stylized by all as "red-necks"? They, too, had a history of peonage, perhaps not in chattel slavery, but also in servitude. If Will were a Christian, is he not responsible to these people?

So, as we have seen, his life took a different course, and some members of the religious-educational establishment, who once praised him, condemned his efforts. His fight for black rights remained unchanged. He only enlarged his private struggle to include the dispossessed white as well—even members of the Ku Klux Klan. Sometimes whether one is labeled a liberal depends upon whose proverbial ox is being gored. It was a supreme irony that once Will Campbell attempted to apply the same Christian principles to "redneck whites" as he had to Southern blacks, some liberals castigated him.

In 1962, Will Campbell's ministry took a new direction after he resigned his position with the National Council of Churches. "A number of my old friends across the South started a 'Save Old Campbell' movement," he remembers. "I was grateful for it, because my family could not survive by farming a few acres of bottomland out here at Mt. Juliet." What saved Campbell and allowed him to practice his guerrilla ministry was the formation of a group known as "the Committee of Southern Churchmen."

"The group had begun in the 1930s as the Fellowship of Southern Churchmen," he said. "I guess you would call them 'Christian Socialists'—Christians who at the time had a socialist political orientation."

Originally the group had gathered during the late Depression years at a mountaintop retreat called Monteagle, south of Nashville. Preachers, labor leaders, schoolteachers, and others gathered in the mountain village, all with a common determination. In a time of economic chaos and political uncertainty, there *must* be a way religion could be taken out of the pulpit and into the streets. Most of the men had been disciples of Reinhold Niebuhr, who had encouraged them to take the gospel out of the pulpit. In fact, survivors of the original Fellowship regard Niebuhr as the spiritual father of their group. In the first meeting on the mountain, although religious and political differences were widespread, there was a common resolve to take the message of Christ into Carolina cotton mills and onto Arkansas tenant farmlands. By 1936, the group had coalesced into the Fellowship of Southern Churchmen. They accepted as their standard of faith the passage from the book of Luke, chapter 5 ". . . To preach the gospel to the poor, to heal the broken-hearted, and recovery of sight to the blind, to set at liberty them that are bruised. . . ."

Those that were bruised . . . They were many in the Depression South, and members of the Committee of Southern Churchmen took separate paths. Howard Kester wandered through the South, helping to organize the Southern Tenant Farmers Union, and fighting for the rights of mill hands and prisoners. In the Cumberland Mountains of Tennessee, Eugene Smathers, a Presbyterian minister, attempted to fashion a model cooperative farm community. During the late 1930s, the group began publishing *Prophetic Religion*, first on a meager budget that allowed only mimeographed copies. Later, the printed magazine spoke of the "hidden church"—in reality, something not hidden at all, but is present on the labor picket lines at Carolina mills or in small meetings of downtrodden Mississippi tenants.

The movement faltered during the years of the Second World War and for two decades afterwards. Perhaps it languished because of similar reasons to the era of American reform in the early 1800s, when those who were committed strove to examine every facet of national ill. As noted by Ralph Waldo Emerson, the marketplace was filled with those demanding reform in *something*—e.g., abolitionism, temperance, diet reform. There was Dorothea Dix and her pleas for the insane, the fanatical Millerites who promised the Second Coming in 1843, and the anti-Catholic societies who sought to improve the New World by struggling against the oncoming waves of Papist immigrants from Ireland and Europe. In their own thinking, all were reformers striving to better society; yet there were simply too many voices in the marketplace.

Perhaps many belonged to the original Fellowship of Southern Churchmen. They all felt the influence of Neibuhr, but each approached the new social gospel differently. Somehow their efforts were weakened by the very diversity of an individualistic Christianity which had first brought them together. The group became fragmented under the stress of its own zeal. One faction gathered in a Tennessee mountain community and organized the Friends of the Soil, a physiocratic return to Thomas Jefferson's principle that those who labor in the soil were God's chosen ones.

In Mississippi, others organized communal societies such as the Delta and Providence Cooperative Farms. Interracial camps sprang up in the Appalachian Mountains of southeastern Virginia and East Tennessee. Other groups fought against lynching, the abuse of mill workers, health problems of the lower South such as hookworm, and other issues.

By the 1950s, an era of middle-class affluence, the Davids of the old Committee of Southern Churchmen had been forgotten. The group remained dormant until the 1960s. "Every year or two they would meet," Campbell recalls, "and talk about the 'old soldier routine.' Oh, we would meet and talk about how everything had gone wrong and about how 'we're going to have a decent funeral because the corpse was starting to smell.' But finally we would decide to meet the next year and keep trying."

Next year was Campbell's departure from the National Council of Churches. The old Fellowship had been revived into a new organization called the Committee of Southern Churchmen.

So began a remarkable publication edited by James Holloway, a native Southerner and, like Campbell, an ordained Baptist minister. Both had attended the divinity school at Yale, but did not meet until they participated in a conference at Georgia's Mercer College in 1961, where Holloway was on the faculty. Since then, Holloway had moved to Berea College in Kentucky where he edits *Katallagete*, while Campbell serves as publisher. The nature of the magazine is symbolic of Campbell's new faith in the years after the admonitions of his friend P. D. East and the tragedy of his brother's death. It is the organ of a guerrilla concern, a holdover from the years of Christian activism in the original Fellowship. *Katallagete*'s subscription list is modest—perhaps 9,000 at best. It does go out—sometimes on an irregular basis—to Catholic nuns, Baptist fundamentalists, agnostics, prominent political figures, prisoners on death row in Southern jails, and many others. The Greek word *katallagete* is derived from St. Paul's charge to the church at Corinth and means, "Be reconciled." This is the center of Will Campbell's vision. Later, in 1970, when Campbell and Holloway co-authored *Up to Our*

Steeples in Politics, St. Paul's admonition was the theme of the book. The book ends with the paraphrase: "Do? *Nothing*. Be? What you are—*reconciled*, to God and man. *Katallagete*."

Even now, Will Campbell is sometimes questioned when he appears on campus seminars. "Somebody is always winding up the session by saying to me, 'Reverend Campbell, you've been telling us here how we ought to forget about the churches and HEW and the NAACP and all the institutions for good. But what are the practical implications of your message? What are you saying to us? It sounds as if you are preaching that we should *do nothing*.' " Campbell smiled. "When I hear that, that is when I know I am getting through to them. That's when I say 'Brothers, now you are finally getting the message. *Do nothing*. Just *be something*. That is the whole message of being a real Christian anyway. Just be what you say you are—a Christian."

Since leaving the National Council of Churches, Campbell's commitment to the principle, "Be reconciled," represents his new calling—even to the extent of ministering to the Ku Klux Klan.

"Sure, I do have several friends who were active in the Klan, and know some people who still are," Campbell said. He smiled wryly. "I am sure the FBI kept a file on me as a left-winger during the days of civil rights activity. Now they keep a file from the other side probably and scratch their heads. 'Who is this guy Campbell? Is he dangerous or just plain crazy?' " Campbell paused from his efforts at rubbing tung oil into a newly carved walking stick. "Oh, I know. Every time I give a lecture somewhere or meet with a room full of divinity professors, somebody asks me, 'Tell me about your work with the Klan.' Hell, I don't have any work with the Klan. Sometimes I try to comfort their families when somebody dies. Maybe preach a funeral." He paused and ran a slender hand down the polished walking stick. "Whenever one of those theologians asks me that, I reply the same way, 'I minister to the Klan by emptying their bedpans.' Isn't that what the Bible teaches—about visiting those who are sick and in prison. I never read there that excludes some black militants or the Klan."

"Besides," he added, "in some way all Americans are in the Klan."

This is one heartbeat of the message of his modern guerrilla ministry. Perhaps it first came to him after the murder of Jonathan Daniels, when P. D. East admonished that we are all bastards loved by God. Maybe this belief grew after his speech at the Chicago civil rights conference in 1961, when his suggestion that black people possessed the same evils as whites—or else they were not equal—drew the anger of the institutional liberal elements. Or it could have been the death of his brother Joe. To Campbell, his brother's tragic end was a symbol of the evils of American civil and religious institutions.

"Technique rules our society," he remarked. "It is a technological concentration camp. If there is a problem, we say we can handle it. International problem? Simply kill thousands of people in Vietnam. Nervous breakdown? Take a tranquilizer. Need religion? Listen to Billy Graham. Or take my brother, Joe. He said 'I have to work hard as a druggist, so I will take a little speed.' Maybe the drugs killed him—but so did institutional thinking."

Or perhaps some of his awakening happened in a 1972 visit to the leader of the "Maoist wing" of the Ku Klux Klan in North Carolina. "Called it that because his group had split from the United States of America, and were considered highly dangerous by the FBI." The Klansman's wife was seriously ill, and Campbell had come to offer comfort. During the evening, Campbell pointedly asked the leader what the Klan stood for. The Klansman replied calmly, "We stand for peace and harmony and freedom."

Campbell smiled as he recalled the incident. "I decided to play a little Socratic game with him, since I was not prepared for that answer. So I asked him to define the terms: what did he mean by peace, harmony, and freedom."

The Klansman shot back "There is a dictionary. Look up the meanings."

"In other words, you Klan people define the words?"

"Sure," the man responded. "What are words—when you use one, it becomes yours."

"All right," Campbell argued, "if the Klan stands for peace, harmony, and freedom, what are the *means* you use to bring it about?"

"Aw," the man replied, "I see what you're getting at. The *means* we are willing to use are murder, torture, threats, blackmail, intimidation, guerrilla warfare, whatever it takes . . ." Then he paused, and Campbell mused later, "I thought I had set the trap."

The Klan leader continued. "Now, preacher, you tell me what we stand for in Vietnam?"

"It took no genius to know who had fallen into a trap," Campbell snorted. "In Vietnam and a lot of places we were a nation of Ku Kluxers, standing for peace, harmony, and the rest—as long as we defined the terms. It didn't even take a Lieutenant Calley to prove the point!"

Later, in a 1973 speech to the Southern Regional Council, he recalled his reconversion to Jesus sounds. He reminisced of his days as a civil rights activist, and admitted "one of the mistakes we made was to take sides . . . because we did not really understand the nature of tragedy."

Steadily, he had come to understand—although not condone—the anger of someone who wore a hooded robe. In another address at a North Carolina seminar on human relations, Campbell drove home his awareness of new Jesus sounds. He spoke of the Klan mentality. "Here is the real tragic figure of the South," he observed. He did not refer to the black man. The black suffered "but he knows why and generally he knows how to suffer." The real victims were Southern poor whites, many of whom came to the New World as indentured servants, bound to their masters for seven years. "Serve me for seven years and I will set you free. But freedom to what, and in what? Freedom to flounder, to drift, to wander west in search of what had been promised but never delivered."

It was a testimony of a new faith which Will Campbell had

acquired after the midday hours of his calling, long after the morning sun along East Fork, or the hot noonday heat on the picket line at Albany, Georgia. It was the credo of P. D. East and his assertion that "We are all bastards." Campbell spoke his faith in the North Carolina address when he spoke of the Klan mentality. "Perhaps I would not feel the pity I do for him if I had not seen and known the resentment of the racist, his hostility, his frustration, his need for someone upon whom to lay blame and punish."

Blame and punish. To Campbell, there was a new awareness that the Southern poor white was also a victim, who had been denied economic advancement, punished by draft regulations, and humiliated by a scornful America. He mused about those, such as the Klan leader in North Carolina: "Maybe I would not feel for him as I do if I had not been so close to him, had not heard his anguished cry when the rains didn't come in time to save his cotton." Perhaps the realization would not have come, "had I not looked upon agony on Christmas Eve night while I, a six-year-old child, feigning sleep, waited for a Santa who would never come."

He had come almost full circle to the childhood memory of East Fork, although, as with the Southern mind, he would never be there again totally.

But he had returned enough to believe that the Ku Klux Klan had selected the wrong enemy. The enemy was not black people, but the institutions which separate and dehumanize people. "I am against violence," he said. "Everyone talks about the big danger of the Klan. My God, who pays that much attention to a poor, small band of uneducated people who burn crosses in cow pastures? Talk about the *real* enemy. Maybe the Klan killed people—hell, we killed hundreds of thousands in Vietnam alone."

Campbell's ministry surfaces in that verse from Second Corinthians: "What I mean is that God was in Christ reconciling the world to himself, no longer holding men's misdeeds against them . . . in Christ's name, we implore you, be reconciled to God!"

"That is what I tell my Klan friends and anybody else who

will listen," Campbell said. "Salvation is really with those people, not with the churches in Nashville and their paved parking
lots. You know, whenever a bunch of Christians has moved from
some brush arbor to an air-conditioned church, they have given
up something they believed about Jesus and never seem to get it
back."

"That is my whole message to the Klan," he continued. 'Be ye
reconciled.' God was in Christ and no longer holds men's shortcomings against them." Campbell glanced off into the hollow at
Mt. Juliet. "You know, that is real good news to a racist, to a
Ku Kluxer who goes around shooting people or burning churches.
The good news is that *this* has been paid for, friend, you don't
have to pay for it."

Some called him J.R., Bob, or "Horse." In 1969, the federal
authorities knew all of his names. J. R. Jones, Grand Dragon of
the North Carolina Ku Klux Klan had been sentenced to a year
in a federal prison. There was to be a small gathering of friends
at his home the evening before he surrendered to officials to begin serving his prison term.

The day before Will and Brenda Campbell were to celebrate
their twenty-third wedding anniversary in the Mt. Juliet hollow.
Campbell planned to fly out the next day to visit Klansman Jones
in North Carolina. A few Klansmen were to gather in the
Dragon's Den to be with Jones before he departed for prison.
Yes, Will Campbell would come to minister to them.

Campbell flew to the Carolina mill city of Greensboro, rented
a car, and drove through another mill town, Salisbury, to the
Dragon's Den. His luggage was simple enough—the guitar case
and the battered suitcase which held a bottle of bourbon. There
was no preaching that night or intonements from the Scriptures,
but it was a religious service. Will Campbell sang for hours the
country songs which view life as a blend of striving and failure—
melodies of broken homes, violent deaths, and unhappy lovers.

Finally he paused. "My last song is coming up," Campbell
said. "I think it is the whole New Testament boiled down into

one song. The message is that it does not matter *what* we have done—Jesus loves us anyway."

"Now," he paused again. "After this song, we're all gonna take communion. So be sure you have a drink in your hands when I finish!"

"You heard that preacher!" a Klan leader shouted. "When we get through we're gonna take communion and we better have a drink in our hands!" The Klansmen rushed for the bottle of bourbon and the kitchen faucet.

Then he sang one last song, in stark, simple lyrics. It told of a man's love for a scarlet woman, and he wanted to take her back to the people who loved her—and to home. Campbell struck a few last chords and then said, "Those who believe Jesus Christ is Lord, let them say *Hallelujah* and drink to his victory!" He laid the guitar aside, reached for the glass of bourbon, and shouted, *"Hallelujah!"* The Klansmen lifted their own glasses, and shouts echoed through the Carolina home.

Later a church staff member in Atlanta scoffed at Campbell's dealings with the white-robed knights. "Do you *really* think you are going to save the souls of the Ku Klux Klan?"

"Maybe not," Campbell shot back. "Maybe they'll save *my* soul!"

Campbell had come, in the years after the long labor in the civil rights crisis, to the essence of his modern guerrilla ministry. He had returned to the ideals of the Reformation, to a personal religion of the catacombs of the early Christians, long before Emperor Constantine proclaimed, in the fourth century, that Christianity would be the religion of the state. Somehow, since then, the state and church as institutions had beaten down good men.

To Campbell the enemy is *any* institution which divides humankind. In government, Campbell wrote, "We are the prisoners of the technological concentration camp which makes war, executes criminals and commits other deeds alien to primitive Christianity." In one speech before the Southern Regional Council, he pronounced a Jeremiah-like condemnation upon the federal state—"You have spies as numerous as the stars in your sky; your CIA and FBI are like locusts, your generals like the hoppers which lie dormant in the walls on a cold day. . . . Your Watergate is a psychological and demonic diversion and ploy, designed in the most sinister grove of your capacity for evil, a pseudoevent to take your mind off what you have really done. Even you cannot face it. Seventy thousand of your young in self-imposed exile rather than carry your banner and claim your name. Forty-five thousand of our finest lie dead for nothing. Millions in Asia no longer live because of you. . . . Your prisons are packed with your poor, your blacks, your undesirables . . . ye who stole a country and killed its inhabitants, ye who sold my black children to build it, fought two global wars to keep it, crushed rebellions in Cuba, Philippines, raped Mexico and all of South America."

Now he moves among all shades of men, but particularly ministers to the low-income whites of the modern South. "They are the most dispossessed people we have," he says. "They have been called rednecks, hillbillies, sand hillers, and many other names. Nobody ever cared for them. Even a slave before the Civil War had some protection."

In the plantation years, there was a sense of paternalism, of the noblesse oblige among the master class. "It was there because of the code of ethics," Campbell asserts. "Here was a South with a religious heritage which was Judeo-Christian, but the system of ethics was Stoic." The Stoic philosophy of the slaveocracy embraced the principles of the Empire of the First Century that sovereignty inhered naturally by compassion—not out of Christian religious faith, but from a sense of duty. Black people were property, to be cared for, because duty demanded it. The code insisted that the master behave justly toward the chattel. "It was a form of truce," Campbell argues. "One between the white master and the black slave. The problem is, there was no room in the alliance for the poor white."

A large number of the Southern population was in this category. As early as 1787, the majority of white adult males in Virginia owned no land. Within four states alone—the Old Dominion, the Carolinas and Georgia, scholars estimate that, by 1860, as many as 400,000 whites lived in abject poverty—almost one fifth of the total population. And in 1850, the estimated rate of white illiteracy in the South was a staggering 20.3 percent, as compared to a low rate of .42 percent in New England.

Here was the root of Campbell's new calling, and of the Jesus sounds he heard later in his career. To understand the man and his message, one must listen to the type of music he delivered that night in the Dragon's Den. He once commented, "I've talked with a lot of people who are interested in the South's culture but look down their noses at country music. I always tell them: if you want to understand the South, go to some country-music concerts and watch. You've got some heavy lines in those songs."

He said this one night when cold winter blasts ripped through the hollow at Mt. Juliet. Campbell stoked the fire in the cast-iron stove as he mused about the contradictions between the life-styles of country-music performers and the God-and-mother image they project. "Maybe these people are just a little more honest," he shrugged. "The singer who goes out and closes his act by singing 'Amazing Grace' doesn't really try to hide what he does back there in the dressing room. I know some other people who close out religious services with whatever the high-church Anglicans close out with and would do the same damned thing shortly after—take a drink or whatever. Just would not admit it."

Campbell's offhand comment is a key factor in understanding the nature of the Southern soul. Perhaps he read the music trade magazine, which boasted two articles by Dolly Parton. In one, she gave credit to God, her "best friend," for success, while in the other she was photographed fondling the outlandish bosom of a life-sized Dolly Parton doll. Or he read the tales of Elvis Presley's drug encounters mingled with his love for religious music. Then, there was Jeanie C. Riley who gained success in Nashville with a lusty song and then testified to her religious faith in the book *Hit the Glory Road*. Something rested beneath the soil of Campbell's mother earth in Middle Tennessee which explained these apparent contradictions, so often presented in themes that appear grotesque. There was some reason for a Jerry Lee Lewis, an alumnus of a fundamentalist Southwestern Bible Institute who became notorious for his hedonistic life-style in country music. Lewis maintained his Pentecostal faith amid the newspaper headlines telling of his involvement with drugs. According to sage Nashville observers, Lewis once balked initially when his producer wanted him to record the song "Great Balls of Fire," because the thematic substance came from a verse in the Bible. The contradictions in country music remain as bizarre as the demented characters in a novel penned by the late Georgia author, Flannery O'Connor.

But there is no real inconsistency in the basic Southern nature or its music. Nor are there genuine hypocrisies in the variances between a Southerner's actions and his religious faith. In the South, religion *is* life—a constant struggle to cope with God, poverty, the long anger produced by the Civil War, and other problems. The basic element in the mind of the South—and its music—is the existence of a civil religion. It is, as we have seen, a complex fabric of religious and regional mythology, which affects views on religion, politics, race, and, above all, the nature of man. The fundamental credo of the South's civil religion is the awareness of man's shortcomings.

There is a deep, mortal quality in Southern piety, which is so creature-oriented that one wonders whether the Creator is viewed as important. The main bulwarks of modern Southern fundamentalist religion—Baptist, Church of Christ, and holiness sects— have much in common. All three faiths began as outposts of loneliness. They were dissenting beliefs which were all condemned by the more conservative religious establishment. They grew initially out of the first important American religious revival—the Great Awakening—in the eighteenth century. The Great Awakening was in part a reaction by frontier people against the dull formalism of more sedate church organizations.

After 1800, the Baptist movement in the South caught fire in the second great upsurge of frontier evangelism, the Great Revival. The movement was a western phenomenon, and those who came forward to the mourner's bench were people with a set of very real fears of Indians, typhoid fever, and milk sickness. After 1800, the American frontier was a brawling, egalitarian society. New states went up on the national flag. There were fortunes to be made in the rich, black-belt cottonlands of Alabama, or on the flat, lonely prairie sod of Illinois. The emotional demands made by loneliness and pestilence joined forces with the individualism of the West. Many American church organizations could not withstand the pressure, and splinter groups arose everywhere along the frontier.

One of the largest, and most enduring, was the Church of Christ. This body broke away from the more rigid Presbyterian establishment, abandoned the concept of original sin, and provided frontiersmen with a new theology that salvation was a bargain between God and man.

The final member of the triumvirate rose in the South after 1900. The Pentecostal movement, with its extreme stress and emotionalism and personal conversion, erupted from a new era of social turmoil in Dixie. The rise of cities, the changing ethics of a new industrial order, and the tension of enduring racial problems all drove many lower income white Southerners to the mourner's bench. They were in a world they could not fathom, but they believed that Jesus could provide the answer. So they abandoned the older churches and formed new sects—the Church of God, Assembly of God, Pentecostal Holiness Church, and a dozen others.

Will Campbell's "parishioners" in the country-music profession come from such deep Southern religious roots. The Southern Baptist faith has produced scores of important names in the music industry, such as Roy Acuff and Hank Williams. The Church of Christ produced Waylon Jennings, Tom T. Hall, and Merle Haggard. Others, such as Johnny Cash, Dolly Parton, and Elvis Presley, came from the depressed culture of the Pentecostal faiths. There are obvious differences in these sectarian beliefs. The Church of Christ stresses a rigid Bible literalism which shuns even the use of instrumental music in worship services. According to this doctrine, no one except its members will achieve salvation. Meanwhile, the Pentecostals emphasize the experienced presence of the supernatural. But these are only surface differences. The religion of country music—and that of much of the South—is one of dislocated people. It concentrates upon the agony of the human condition, and contains a fierce individualism. Man is central. Religion is a compact between God and mortals, and is an exercise of free will.

There are some elements in this faith which tell a great deal about the Southern mind and its music. One is the peculiar arrangement of a Southerner's concept of the Trinity. It is not composed of God, Jesus, and the Holy Spirit, as some Christians would maintain. Their Trinity is God, Man, and the Devil (sometimes one wonders if God is not outnumbered).

Satan is an agent of failure in the modern South as well. He is regarded as a real being cast from Heaven—an elusive creature whom Dixie preachers have described in St. Peter's words as "the roaring lion"; he is the rationale of broken marriages, alcoholism, and all other human defects. To a Southerner, Satan is also a spirit that lives *within* the person. He is part of the inner Southern soul, and attempts to shape passions.

The irony is that in the fundamentalist ethos of the Trinity, God becomes the outsider—a concept which probably has done much to engender further feelings of alienation and insecurity in the Southern mind. When a country singer delivers a religious hymn such as "Who At the Door Is Standing?," he expresses the fact that, initially, man is estranged from God. The Creator remains on the outside, inviting a Southerner to accept His principles. He may enter—or send the emissary Jesus—but only at the will of the listener.

In brief, a Southerner is always part of his religious experience, and every act is related at least in part to his theology. Marriage, drinking, infidelity, earning wages are all part of a relationship between man, God, and Satan. A devout churchman would contend that inner feelings are influenced by the presence of Lucifer. A liberal theologian would insist that Satan is an exaggerated personification of the natural passions of sex, anger, or the more abnormal feelings of violence.

Will Campbell understands that the only sure thing in this concept of the Trinity is the tragedy of human existence. Man is caught somewhere between the pulpit intonements and his own desires. Life is, at best, a transient existence where failure is always present.

Campbell's belief in a primitive Christian faith is based on his awareness of the civil religion of the South. His constant urging, "Be reconciled," is an admission of human failure. By the evening of his life he has also come to the realization that a deep human compassion exists within Southern folkways. The very statement appears to be a contradiction. The South's record of intolerance is well documented—slavery, lynch mobs in Amite County, anti-Catholic sermons in Nashville's Protestant bulwarks even in the 1960s when John Kennedy sought the Presidency, anti-Semitic literature distributed by white-robed Klansman, Governor Ross Barnett standing in the doorway at Ole Miss to deny enrollment to a black man, the murders at Philadelphia, Mississippi. Campbell has seen all this and more—the grim remembrances of fear, frustration, and anger, the disenfranchised black pitted against the downtrodden white.

"Somewhere down the road, I learned that Southern people had a special compassion," Campbell insists. "Maybe part of my awareness came when I moved out to this old farm," he recalled. After all, the local Mt. Juliet community did not know how to take a Will Campbell. There were tales of his work in the civil rights movement, of how he marched at Little Rock and had been a friend to Martin Luther King, Jr. Other stories told of his relationship with the Ku Klux Klan. "Nobody quite knew what I was," he said. "But two incidents stuck with me after we bought this old farm. One night a local boy came out to do some electrical work in the log office. He was up on a ladder fiddling with some wiring, when he turned to me and said, 'Now, I've heard all kinds of stories about you. Just what do you do?' "

The question gave Campbell pause and he proceeded to explain something of his work with the Committee of Southern Churchmen, of how, yes, he had worked with the civil rights movement, and yes, again, he had ministered to people in the Ku Klux Klan. Then the man on the ladder grinned, and mumbled, "You know, frankly I don't give a damn *what* you do." "You could not improve on that answer," Campbell recalled.

Another time, some local residents were drinking beer in a nearby tavern. One fondled his beer can and talked about this newcomer in the community. "I hear this fellow was big in the civil rights business," he commented. "Hear he was in those protest marches." A burly fellow who had come to know Preacher Will Campbell edged up beside him. "Hoss, let me tell you." He stared at the other man. "I don't give a damn *what* he believes. I know he believes in *something* and that's good enough for me."

The irony is that there has always been far more human tolerance in the civil religion Campbell preaches, than in the formal Christian institutions of the Southern heritage. So it was not strange that Will Campbell discovered in country music a far deeper compassion for human frailty than existed in the Southern fundamentalist religious heritage of the singers. Nashville's lyrics stress man's plight of existing somewhere between the good and the bad. Dolly Parton was educated in her grandfather's Holiness church in the Great Smokies. It's no wonder she would write and record a song like "The Seeker," in which the singer describes herself as the "bad seed" and "the loser," yearning for Jesus to show the way. Meanwhile, Johnny Paycheck, one of Nashville's outlaw types, sings "I'm the Only Hell My Mamma Ever Raised." The hero in the song steals license plates, commits armed robbery, and ends up in prison—but he still misses Mamma and can mumble a few words from the country gospel number "Precious Memories."

Yet there is something else in country music which explains better why it contains a deep sense of compassion. "I remember how I became so involved with these people," he recalls. "It was back in the late 1950s, after I had moved to Nashville to work for the National Council of Churches. Back then, of course, I would *deny* liking country music. That was not the thing that a liberal was supposed to say.

"Hell, if I had admitted it," Campbell said, "country music already had made a deep impression. I remember a time riding an airplane to some civil rights conference, and I sat next to a singer named Hank Snow. I recognized him and we started talking about music. I kept insisting to him that I didn't *know* much about country music, but proceeded to name about every song he had ever recorded. He smiled and said 'Sounds like you know a lot about the music.' "

What Campbell did not know came later when he opened his Nashville office within the confines of Music Row.

"Next door to my office there was this rooming house. There was this young fellow there who had come to Nashville to make his way, and he worked as bartender, janitor, whatever, to pay his board. His name was Kris Kristofferson. We got to know each other. He became curious about what I did, and I was just as puzzled as to what *he* did. So he would come over to my old office and talk. Sometimes he would bring his guitar and sing, or play the one I kept in the corner.

"I learned a lot from that first encounter about the South, and life, and Nashville," Campbell mused. "Part of it is what I say often—that those singers were the real poets who tell truths about life. And part of the learning was to realize that there is something deeper in the Southern soul than those formal church institutions like the one I worked for."

In the years to come, a country song like the "Outlaw's Prayer" would hold meaning for Will Campbell. The lyrics might appear at first hearing to be almost ludicrous. It is a recitation uttered with the background strains of the gospel tune, "Sweet Hour of Prayer." It concerns a country singer on tour who becomes lonely on a Sunday morning, and wanders into a large, ornate church building. He is rejected because of his weird clothing and unkempt appearance, and he proceeds to contrast the well-dressed deacons inside the lavish structure with Jesus' band of ragged followers. The moral is obvious. The singer, with his beard, unorthodox clothing, and fundamental honesty, is more akin to the throngs who heard the Sermon on the Mount than are the businessmen inside the church building.

The lyrics and presentation are deceptively simple. Beneath the sentimentality is a more important reason for the strong feeling for humanity one senses in country music. In "The Outlaw's Prayer," the singer-hero yearns to share again his early religious experience, but finds that he is socially unacceptable in a Southern community, even when he tries to attend church. Why is he an outcast? If the singer were raised a good Baptist or Pentecostal, his religious indoctrination on man's good and bad nature would be the same as the others. But he left that culture while relatives and friends remained. They continued to hold firmly to that peculiar cultural alchemy of family, home, and church. Their survival was within their world, not in an outside one filled with the enemy described by pulpit orators every Sunday—sexual immorality, alcoholism, and drugs.

Elvis Presley, Johnny Cash, Carl Perkins, Jerry Lee Lewis, Tom T. Hall, Waylon Jennings, and a hundred others fit a pattern. Most of them were probably always considered misfits by local religious leaders. They wore long hair or different clothes, and did not settle down in the good Calvinist mold of getting a steady job and raising children. They played music in roadside taverns, bars, and at dances. They played in combos, bluegrass groups, or honky-tonk country bands. They stayed up later than other people, and slept late in the morning. Meanwhile, people asked them why they did not "get a regular job like everyone else." They were not like everyone else, even if they shared the same beginnings.

Country music is based on human frailty and a tolerance for those who transgress. Much of it comes from writers and performers who grew up on the other side of town. Merle Haggard's song "If We Make It Through December!" is a simple tale of a blue-collar worker with children and a tight budget, who was laid off as the Christmas season approached. One does not have to serve time in San Quentin, as Haggard did, to understand the song.

Dolly Parton's "Coat of Many Colors" (a word-play on the Old Testament saga of Joseph and his brothers) told of a poor country girl who was ridiculed by schoolmates for wearing ragtag clothing. Songwriter Bob McDill's "Rednecks, White Sox and Blue Ribbon Beer" is more than a whimsical scenario of a few minutes in a roadside tavern. The cowboy playing the jukebox, the crowd in white socks which assembles at twilight, the mean drunk in the corner, the waitress whose hard face still bears sex appeal—all represent a culture of lonely people who suffer the additional burden of awareness that others view them as rednecks.

Sometimes Will Campbell expresses this sentiment in late-night music sessions in the old kitchen on the farm at Mt. Juliet. A few friends from nearby farms or mobile homes drift in. They sip bourbon around the circular kitchen table and listen to Brother Will preach the word. The word can be a country song called "Kay."

"Kay" is a simple hymn of Southern civil religion. If one takes the few bare lyric stanzas and builds upon them, the end result is a composite of the Southern faith. A taxi driver on lower Broad Street loved a girl who lived in a cheap boardinghouse, probably out on Sixteenth Avenue. She came to Nashville, hopeful of a career as a singer. The cab driver encouraged her, probably bought her Blue Plate specials at Linebaugh's Cafe below Fifth Avenue, and drove her across the Viaduct by Union Station to the Music Row section on West End. No doubt he took her there dozens of times, and waited for her in his cab parked on Sixteenth Avenue. To pass the time, he watched the Jesus freaks amble past on their way to a dingy room called home up near Belmont College. A Vanderbilt coed strolled by in a pair of genuine, expensive Levi's. Then the cabbie watched two aspiring musicians unwind in a dirty 1957 Plymouth with Georgia plates. They had the proper trappings—Texas hats, long hair, flowered shirts, and Woolworth's best neckchains. God only knew if they had the talent and the Nashville connections. Somehow "Kay" made these connections. She no longer needed her taxi-driver lover for trips to Music Row. Some man in a Mercedes picked her up now. There were no more meatloaf dinners at Linebaugh's. Now she was dining at Mario's on West End. The first single release from her new album received a lot of air play and the taxi driver read about her in fan magazines.

He never spent time with her now. Once, when he dropped off a pair of Michigan tourists at the chain of nightspots on Printer's Alley, below Fourth Avenue, he spotted her walking out of Boots Randolph's place with the dude and some other well-heeled friends. He waved, but her only response was a quick, nervous half-smile, and she glanced aside to see if her friends had noticed even that feeble response. He drove down lower Church Street, then turned up Third Avenue. It was Saturday night, and the radio was alive with country music. He heard her new hit record several times, while he ferried an assortment of people: the two soldiers from Fort Campbell who never stopped telling war stories; the pregnant girl who must be rushed to General Hospital; and the businessman who dropped a twenty-dollar bill on the front seat and asked the driver to find a little action.

There is more feeling in "Kay" than one could find in a Southern Baptist hymn. The cab drivers and Kays somehow find their way to the hollow at Mt. Juliet as do many more stray souls. Once in a feature study of Will Campbell in *Life* magazine, Marshall Frady wrote a long article which he called "Fighter for Forgotten Men." It is hard to improve on that description. The old guest-quarters on the hill—the Dolan house—or the confines of Campbell's log office have witnessed a cross-section of humanity—theologians, country musicians, black militants, Pulitzer Prize authors, and local factory workers. One day the telephone rang in Campbell's home and he went into another room to take the call. When he returned to the round oak table in the kitchen, someone asked, "Who was that?" "Somebody," he murmured. "She just wanted to cry."

Campbell's status as the hero of modern Southern folk religion troubles him. Part of his irritation comes from the tendency to affix a label to what he does. "Some people call me a counselor," Campbell complains. "I don't know why, because it's such an arrogant concept, that I just don't use it. I'm not a counselor— don't want to be a counselor." He paused and recalled an incident in the 1970s when Duke University invited him to serve as theologian-in-residence. Campbell accepted the post, but insisted, "I am not a theologian." When he arrived on campus, local newspapers and other media advertised the presence of Will Campbell as theologian-in-residence. He complained, half in jest, of how the divinity school had broken their word. "But you are *our* kind of theologian," one official insisted. Campbell retorted, "You have been so brainwashed by the language that you think you are flattering me. That's like saying 'You're not like the rest of the Jews; you're a good guy. You're our kind of Jew.' Theologians are scholarly people who write papers for one another, footnote them, and publish them in journals. That's not what I am. I'm just a preacher."

Sometimes even being a preacher can produce tremendous demands upon Campbell's already heavy schedule. Amidst his frequent lectures, running a farm, working for the Committee of Southern Churchmen, writing books and articles, laboring with the Southern Prison Ministry, being a social activist, Campbell has managed to find time for scores of people who come to the Hollow. "I'm going to have to limit my time," he admits. "It can get out of hand."

"Accept it," someone once told him. "You *are* a folk hero."

He is, but refuses to acknowledge it. "I am not a folk hero," Campbell insists, "and have always prided myself—sort of an arrogant pride—in stopping that. People need cult figures. And if they want them, they'll build them."

"What do you mean?" his friend asked.

"For years, I have received letters from seminarians. Every year they would write—this was particularly true in the 1960s— they would say 'We're going to take a year off from formal study

and want to come down South and do what you guys do.' "
Campbell would respond simply, "Well, what do we guys do?"
" 'Well, you know,' they would respond. 'I'm interested in race
and prison problems and that sort of thing.' " "Well," Campbell
retorted, "don't you have any black people or prisons where *you*
live? 'Yeah, uh, we do, but you see . . .' they would hesitate."
"Oh, I see," Campbell would reply. "You want to be my disciple. 'Yeah, that's it.' Well tough shit. I'm trying to *be* a disciple.
I don't want any disciples. I look back and see a bunch of people
following me and I fall to pieces.

"Which," Campbell recalled later, "is the distinction between
being a guru or cult figure and not being one of those things.
The guru says, 'Yes, come on down. We have this program and
we'll put you to work.' I've never done that. It's dangerous. Soon
you start believing that shit."

Others seem to believe it. Each day a hefty sack of letters
arrive in the mailbox on the farm road, and the telephone rings
constantly. "There was this guy in North Carolina who sent me
a long list of questions about my beliefs. He said if I didn't answer them, he would hitchhike to Mt. Juliet and take up four
hours of my time. There was another one who wrote from
Louisville, Kentucky. He said he had been a fan of mine, had
read *Brother to a Dragonfly* three times and 'I understand you receive callers.' "

Campbell does receive callers, often in the early morning hours.
"But at some point you have to say that's it," he said. "I've got
all the people I can relate to. Now I know that sounds like I'm
saying 'I'm important and don't have time for you.' Maybe that's
true. I don't have time for you. I'm just one Marine and that's
all. I don't have a big staff, social secretary, assistant pastor, or
any hot-shot specialists to give you a battery of tests. I just can't
handle any more ministry—don't even like that word ministry—
than I have now. Sometimes people just show up, stop out on
the highway and call me here at the farm wanting to come over."

Will Campbell lets them come. Together they sit in the kitchen
or out in the log office. Sometimes a bottle of bourbon is passed

around. More often, Will Campbell works to put their lives back together, talking around chews of tobacco, always on his eternal of country music.

To Will Campbell, it *is* religious music of the soul of the South. This is why he lives in Nashville, delivering country-music songs in sermons and lectures. It also explains why, of all the lost sheep who find their way to Campbell's hollow, the musicians are special people. They are *aberrations*—total exaggerations of the guilt, alienation, and feelings of divided loyalties which were his own heritage.

The contradictions between life as it *was* and it *is* are awesome strains on the mentality of country musicians. For them Nashville is a total culture shock, and even after they live there for a while, the contrasts between their past and present life-styles are almost incredible. No more stinking outdoor toilets, rundown frame homes without screens, or front yards filled with derelict automobiles and the putrid scent of oil and grease. No more church box-suppers, family reunions, or bull sessions at the local Western Auto store, where a creative, sensitive person stares at his brother and four children, and ponders "My God, ten years from now, is this where I'll be?" And no more sweatshop hours in cotton gins, hardware stores, gasoline stations, or tobacco barns.

Here is the genesis of that massive insecurity one encounters in Nashville. The chasm between past and present life-styles is grotesque.

Five years ago, a singer worked in a mill during the day, sang in roadhouses at night, and still brought home only one-hundred-and-fifty dollars a week. Now he grosses several thousand dollars for a single concert. He came to Nashville in a shabby Plymouth but now can afford a pair of Mercedes with ease. His early starving days in Nashville meant surviving in a trailer court on the Nolensville Pike, but now he lives alongside the insurance executives in Belle Meade or Brentwood.

It's *not* merely the rapid change in fortune, though that is massive enough. The difficulty arises when one attempts to reason out the transition from beauty operator or pulpwood cutter to superstar. Normal Southern life—if there is such a thing—is unreal enough with its paradoxes of religion and violence, beautiful countryside and fields of rusty automobiles, graceful mansions, and hovels beset by mosquitoes and hookworm.

Back home in some drab Alabama village, the singer's brother and sister-in-law—call them Brenda and Ronnie—are never confronted with paradoxes in their own lives. This is in part because most Southerners never really do. As novelist Robert Penn Warren observed, there is a strong resistance to analysis in the mind of the South. More important, Ronnie and Brenda in the Alabama village can accept the contradictions in their lives with more ease because the contrast between what they are and aspire to be is not immense. They still belong to a tightly woven structure of family, community, and time which changes little. Perhaps Brenda was the high school cheerleader and Ronnie the football quarterback on the county high-school team.

Ten years for them bring little change. They still occupy a pew at the Baptist church, have the same basic circle of friends, and are interlocked in a family circle. Their mobility is confined to a local area. They first lived in a rented mobile home, then moved to a white frame house in an older section. When black people moved in they moved to a ranch-type home with a carport and a few maple saplings wired on the front lawn. They are still there close to the root of their being, and experience only aging and the change in economic status.

Meanwhile, their relative in Nashville, the successful musician or songwriter, also has roots, and feels the awesome contrast between past and present. Success in the country-music culture conveys a sense of power not known in the old life. From the lower economic stratum of Dixie society, the singer moves into the plush neighborhoods of Oak Hill or Brentwood. His neighbors are physicians and attorneys. The Maryland Farms club or various country clubs welcome his membership, while local banks maintain special investment arrangements for his money.

His former drab life was the Southern Baptist hymnal and

shabby pianos in rural churches. It was consisted of singing at local funerals, playing a mail-order guitar on the front porch, or performing at schoolhouse suppers or small-town theaters which reeked of stale popcorn. The media—radio, television, and fan magazines—remind him of his star status; when these fail, a loyal cadre of hangers-on are there to reinforce his ego. The singer now has more than he dreamed of during those lean years.

When singers come to seek counsel from Will Campbell, he understands their love-hate feelings, the dichotomies between their past and present. "Living in Nashville makes it worse for them," Campbell observed. "After all, Nashville is the absolute exaggeration of the surface contradictions in the Southern soul."

If the capital of country music were in Atlanta or New Orleans, a heavy dose of guilt would still pervade the music because of its Southern Protestant heritage. Living in Nashville only makes matters worse. Nobody, as we have seen, can escape religion in Nashville. The telephone directory's yellow pages are filled with advertisements for hundreds of churches. Saturday newspapers have lists of announcements of Sunday goings-on. One can scarcely drive along a city street without passing a church parking lot with a couple of buses. Local television, billboard advertising, and radio programs are full of religious subjects. The musicians have to live in this environment and Nashville continually reminds them of that sin-based mentality they had attempted to escape. There is no cutoff point. Other elements followed them to Nashville, brought by their white-collar neighbors from the surrounding rural counties. They build huge church buildings, buy fleets of buses, and publish religious tracts.

Perhaps it was symbolic that the first musician befriended by Will Campbell in Nashville was writer-singer Kris Kristofferson. Sometimes in the old farmhouse kitchen, while celebrating communion with friends over glasses of bourbon, or even in academic lecture halls, Will Campbell will deliver a Kristofferson melody, "Sunday Morning Coming Down," which explains much of the paradox of the Southern soul. Many lonely people who found their way to Nashville, hoping for a niche in the music trade, can identify with the teller of the tale. He is an aspiring singer who survives in a sleazy boardinghouse room which reeks of cigarette smoke and stale beer. He stumbles out onto the sidewalks of Nashville on a Sunday morning, to become aware of home and how far away his roots are.

Sunday anywhere in the Protestant South is hell for those who live outside the mainstream of middle-America, but is far worse in Nashville. Religious groups seize radio stations and remind everyone that Sunday belongs to the Lord. Church marquees bear family slogans and bumper stickers inform tailgaters that the explanation for a broken home is simple—not enough family prayer. Somehow, during the week, the contrasts between the predominant religious-business social fabric of Nashville and the Ishmaels of Music Row are buffered by the crowds and traffic along Church Street and in shopping malls such as Hundred Oaks and Madison Square.

Then comes Saturday, the religious-business bloc folds its tents and retreats into Oak Hill or West Meade, giving up the city for twenty-four hours to the music crowd. Pickup trucks from Alabama and camper vans from Indiana prowl the old Lower Broad district where Hank Williams raised hell. These visitors gawk at exhibits in the Country Music Hall of Fame, and shuffle down to the old Ryman Auditorium to snap a few instamatic photographs. They want to eat breakfast at Linebaugh's Cafe where Roy Acuff dined, or purchase a photograph of singer Conway Twitty in a gilded plastic frame. By nightfall, the city belongs to country music. Thousands gather at Opryland to cheer on such performers as Bill Monroe and the Bluegrass Boys. Others are already rambling the narrow Printer's Alley between Third and Fourth avenues. Elsewhere, down on Lower Broad, hardcore music fans roam through Tootsie's Orchid Lounge. Out on Elliston Place, the beer flows in the Gold Rush and the Exit-Inn, where Vanderbilt students, urban music enthusiasts, and youthful musicians hopeful of discovery are gathered. Nashville on a Saturday night is one vast crushed beer can. . . .

On a Sunday morning, vomit, Jim Beam bottles, and Blue

Ribbon cans litter Printer's Alley, Lower Broad, and Elliston Place. The long-legged, booted young prostitutes with the expressionless faces are wrapping up business on Fourth Avenue. Somewhere out along the fringes of Music Row, in the Belmont and Hillsboro districts, the young music hopefuls who came to Nashville with beaded shirts and worn suitcases are sleeping off the booze and pot.

While the music crowd slumbers, the church-business complex recaptures the city. The local telephone directory boasts nine yellow pages of church advertisements; all nine pages have church buses out on Nashville's streets, prowling the highways and hedges to bring in the sinners to massive tabernacles such as First Baptist on Broad Street or Madison Church of Christ out on Gallatin Road. Television and radio stations are clogged with local ministers damning well-nigh everything the music industry talks about—sex without marriage, drinking, and divorce.

Sometimes Will Campbell sings another Kris Kristofferson melody which is another hymn of the South's civil religion. Perhaps it is an autobiography of the young Rhodes Scholar Kristofferson who wanted to be a Nashville songwriter. He came to Campbell's town, worked as a bartender and janitor, and wrote his music. At first, in the days when Kristofferson met Campbell, the young writer was financially destitute and his marriage had fallen apart. Then someone began recording his songs, and Kristofferson himself became a successful singer, eventually earning a fortune. Long after much of this happened, he wrote the song "Why Me, Lord?" which pondered why someone like himself deserved the good things.

"I understand how the singers feel," Campbell said. "Here they are, living in some big house out on the south side of Nashville. Meanwhile their old buddies are still back in the home town, trying to make a living in some gasoline station. Maybe they are small-time musicians who wanted to make it big in Nashville, too. Ever read one of those articles on what happens to people who survive some disaster like an airplane crash—how they keep torturing themselves with the question 'Why did I survive and other people didn't?' It's the same thing. A singer has a lot of chart records and now he wonders why he made it and his friends are still back in some small Alabama town."

It was not just the singers who wonder "Why Me, Lord?" Will Campbell does the same. "Why was I the one chosen to leave Amite County? I don't know. Why was I different? Why didn't I join the Klan? Why did I want to march at Little Rock, or even go off to Yale Divinity School instead of staying in the Mississippi Delta?"

In the late night hours, Will Campbell strums the guitar and sings melodies of Southern guilt. Sometimes it is "Lucille," about a man standing shamefaced in a Toledo hotel room with the naked wife who had deserted her farmer husband and children. Or it is "Goodhearted Woman," a ballad of remorse for the loving wife who endures a man's rakish ways. Sometimes it is "Mamma Tried," a poignant melody of a convict's guilt when he recalled his mother's efforts to train him the right way.

What the singer in Nashville does with these feelings of guilt and alienation is almost a microcosm of the entire Southern experience. Some remain within the steepled churches which Campbell cries out against. Meanwhile the new evangelism which swept across America in the late 1970s has captured others. At least fifty million Americans claim to have been "born again." Old-time religion has become a multimillion-dollar concern that has touched the lives of every social and economic strata—politicians, suburban housewives, rock singers, even Black Panther leader Eldridge Cleaver. Bumper stickers on the road claim "I Found It," the Christian Broadcast Network beams testimonials of faith to millions each day, and over two thousand media preachers broadcast every week.

Over five million of the new evangelicals are involved in the charismatic revival. It is a phenomenon which cuts across socioeconomic lines, and involves everyone from college professors to millworkers. Some refer to it as "neo-Pentecostalism," because it boasts many of the beliefs of the older Southern holiness sects.

There is the same conviction that the Holy Spirit enters one's body and bestows special gifts—the ability to heal, prophesy, and speak in strange tongues. There is also the same faith in the millenium—that Jesus will return victorious to earth and reign as a mortal for a thousand years.

Joining such groups is a form of reconversion, or returning to an earlier point in one's cultural background. Most musicians cannot go back that far. They have been away too long from the dingy Alabama holiness church buildings, the sweaty preachers in frayed white shirts and shiny blue suits, and the groaning of earnest souls seeking to drive Satan from their lives. They cannot return to the smug, red-brick Baptist citadels of East Texas, or to the drabness of the box suppers and courthouse square bull sessions.

But such things are still there. Those impregnable Southern roots of home and community are never really severed. The old hymns are still familiar, even on a performer's Sunday spent on a monotonous highway between engagements. The musicians talk about religion even more than they probably realize, and in their frequent jam sessions, the old Carter Family gospel tunes are often played. Most still believe in heaven and hell, and in the redeeming blood of Jesus. Even if they didn't, the ever-present Nashville religious culture stares at them from every streetcorner, reminding them always of their past.

They are all still trying to cope with both their Southern heritage and the unique strains of the music culture. Salvation for them can be anything which relieves anxiety and loneliness. It can be hit records, pills, lavish homes, or glasses of bourbon. Often it can be a visit to Will Campbell's farm in search of guidance.

In the old farmhouse off the highway, Campbell listens to them into the late hours on until daylight hits the rocky hills.

EPILOGUE

Will Campbell went to Gass's Grocery often, until the creeping suburban patterns of Nashville finally engulfed it. He went during nights in midweek when he returned from visiting a death-row prisoner, or from a lecture on a university campus; other times, on Friday evenings.

It was a combination country store, cafe, and tavern—and, perhaps, a church as well. Most of the people who came to Gass's Grocery at night were the alienated and uprooted—farm people but not rural people. Many had deep roots in the bluegrass plain of Middle Tennessee, but economic change had forced them from the plow to jobs in Nashville factories.

At night the parking lot at Gass's Grocery was filled with trucks and fast, sleek automobiles such as Trans-Ams and Camarros. Some were people who had grown up in the village of Mt. Juliet, once a hamlet isolated from even the contradictions of Nashville, but the growing population brought about a suburban invasion of the country village. Inside the smoke-filled, combination bar and restaurant were Will Campbell's people.

Most of them were home, but not home at all. They had been nurtured in the staunch fundamentalist religious faiths of the Nashville plain. Now they were trapped, as all Southerners are, in the love-hate relationship between past and present. The old world had given them something positive which had been re-tained—a love for the soil, for the deep roots of heritage and memory. Even the stubborn limestone outcroppings at Mt. Juliet provoked fierce love for the Nashville basin, and so they lived on small farms or in modest mobile homes, and drove long distances to work in town. Yet their staunch religious upbringing had not prepared them for the real pressures of life: alcohol, infidelity, divorce, and financial turmoil.

Sometimes the crowd sat and drank beer, or fed money into the jukebox. More often, they brought musical instruments. In loud, boisterous fashion guitars would be tuned. Then someone would shout, "Let Will Campbell start a number!"

The crowds always would fall silent as Will Campbell began to sing. Often he delivered "Storms Never Last, Do They Baby?" a lyric lament of a married couple determined to endure through their troubles. Or maybe, again, it was "Rednecks, White Sox and Blue Ribbon Beer," which bespoke the feelings of a confused, transient society, not unlike the crowd in the tavern at Mt. Juliet, who were somewhere between the farm and middle-American suburbia.

They were hymns of a faith, of a realization in the Southern soul that man strives but fails often. Deep within the hard guitar licks and Will Campbell's strong yet soft voice was the resignation that decades before took root in Amite County.

Sometimes Will Campbell ended his impromptu concert with a famous country song penned by writer Bob McDill, "Good Ole Boys Like Me." It is a favorite of Will Campbell's, because it gives life to his faith, to the awareness of the contradictions within the soul of his land. The song tells of a child who was trundled to bed under a picture of Stonewall Jackson; of how the father would stagger into the modest bedroom, with gin on his breath and a Bible in his hand, to tuck in his son. Then came the years of growing up and the attempt to escape the futility of small-town rural life. The balladeer spoke of how he watched friends burn themselves out while he escaped from the confines of his roots; yet he remained always part of the Southern community of believers. He kept coming back in the chorus, where he told of the sound of wind in the live oak trees, and of how the Williams boys—singer Hank and writer Tennessee—were dear to his world of contradictions. Near the end, Will Campbell concluded that we are all what we are going to be. In the last refrain, he asked the unanswerable question, "So what do you do with good ole boys like me?"

It was a Jesus sound which reached far back to the Glory Hole in Amite County.